Determined Survivors

Determined Survivors

Community Life
among the Urban Elderly

Janice A. Smithers

Rutgers University Press
New Brunswick, New Jersey

Library of Congress Cataloging in Publication Data

Smithers, Janice A., 1931–
   Determined survivors.

   Bibliography: p.
   Includes index.
     1. Retirement communities—California—Los Angeles—
Case studies. 2. Aged–California—Los Angeles—Case
studies. 3. Single people—California—Los Angeles—
Case studies. I. Title.
   HQ1063.S595   1985   305.2'6'0979494   84–17794
   ISBN 0–8135–1079–1
   ISBN 0–8135–1080–5 (pbk.)

48, 117

To my family and the residents of the St. Regis

Contents

Figures

Tables

Acknowledgments

Many people contributed to this work, but it is to the elderly residents of the St. Regis that I owe my deepest debt of gratitude for giving me the privilege of entering their private lives as a friend and confidante. I was a stranger in their world, and yet they welcomed me with friendship and good will. Their courage and tenacity in the face of difficult odds and their resourcefulness in helping one another during critical times exemplified in the highest degree the human will to survive.

Other counselors who worked with me at the St. Regis also provided valuable assistance during the course of the study. In particular, Joan Thompson and Dorothy Leichner contributed insightful observations gained from their experiences in working with the tenants. The study of the St. Regis would not have been possible without the permission and cooperation of the Housing Authority. Their staff members enabled me to gain a deeper understanding of the numerous problems involved in the day-to-day management of facilities of this kind, and I was privileged to witness many instances of their caring and concern for the tenants.

A special debt of gratitude goes to my valued friend and colleague Dr. Jacqueline Goodchilds. Her editing skills and intellectual insights contributed immeasurably to the form and quality of the work. Most important of all, she provided the necessary moral support that kept me at the task during the long months of revisions. In addition, I also want to thank Dr. Robert Emerson, the chairperson of my doctoral committee, who provided many hours of discussion and guidance during my work on an earlier version of the manuscript. I am also indebted to Dr. Melvin Seeman, Dr. David Lopez, Dr. Nathan Cohen, and Dr. Yung-Huo Liu for their assistance and helpful comments. And lastly, my thanks go to my husband, my mother, and my children, whose love and support ultimately made this book possible. The final manuscript was expertly typed by Margaret Thomlinson.

Introduction

This book is a study of survivorship in old age. Specifically, the focus is on the survival challenges confronting a group of elderly men and women living in single apartment units at the St. Regis, an age-segregated, high-rise public housing project in the inner city of Los Angeles. Common themes emerge, however, that transcend differences in socioeconomic status and personal circumstances. To be old is to be socially marginal in a society that prizes the vigors of youth in contrast to the wrinkles and reduced capacities of later life. Thus the challenge in old age is to remain socially viable—to preserve a valued life style in preferred surroundings in spite of losses in income, health, and available support systems.

Indeed, differences exist both in the coping skills that we use and in the personal and social resources we have with which to counter the alterations in life circumstances we all must face. Finances determine the quality of medical care, housing, and recreation. Family and friendship networks influence the amount of supportive care available in time of need; personal ability to contend with crises such as health losses and changes in residence varies according to lifelong coping patterns. Whether the focus is on community life in a life-care home, an affluent condominium complex, or a mobile home park or on the efforts of elderly people to remain in their communities of origin, the primary issue is maintaining independence within the constraints of the cumulative changes that are inevitable in the process of growing old.

Selecting a retirement community for single, aged people, in downtown Los Angeles as a site for my research was a consequence of a sociological interest in the diversity and quality of life experienced in these settings and also of my own personal concerns about increasing age. I have witnessed the courage and determination of my mother who, in her late seventies, was faced with the task of caring for my father during the last stages of a terminal illness that lasted for several years. His abiding wish was to die in his own bed and avoid the dehumanizing experience of institutional placement. This was accomplished through my mother's nursing skills, her loving care, and the involvement of outside support systems consisting of health professionals and concerned relatives. Her comment to me at the time of his death was that he was able to "die with dignity." Her capacities honed over years of experience as the family caretaker and her devotion of my father's well-being made possible the fulfillment of his last wish. Since his death, she has remained in the family home. In spite of physical ailments and reduced energy, she has steadfastly resisted any suggestions by her children that she move into a more convenient apartment or have a live-in companion. "I can look after myself," she replies, "and I will stay here until they carry me out." What kind of a survivor will I be in my old age? Will I be able to function as well under similar or different circumstances? These are the kinds of questions that motivated me, in part, to undertake a study of ways in which older people meet the survival challenges of later life.

I also reviewed several studies of retirement communities including Hochschild's (1973) excellent appraisal of community formation among a group of elderly widows residing in a public housing project in the San Francisco area and Ross's (1977) insightful work analyzing the emerging social organization in a newly built retirement facility for Parisian construction workers and their families. In particular, I was interested in the investigations of the support systems and quality of life of aged people living alone in the inner city. As a long-term resident of the Los Angeles area, I have been intrigued by the kaleidoscopic character of street life in the heart of the metropolitan center, the contrasts between shiny glass skyscrapers filled with purposeful activity and turn-of-the-century churches attempting to justify their existence in spite of dwindling congregations and small coffers. And I have noticed unusual numbers of elderly walking slowly along city streets, sitting quietly on porches of old rooming houses, and feeding pigeons in Pershing Square. Where did they come from? Were they recent arrivals on the urban scene who gravitated there to find inexpensive living more in accord with small pension checks? Did their lifestyles typically reflect the kind of social isolation described in several studies of SRO (single-room occupancy)[1] living in dilapidated downtown hotels? Given the realities of high crime rates and deteriorating housing, it was difficult for me to conceive how anyone, especially the aged, would live in the central city by choice. To answer some of these questions, I found myself delving further into literature on lifestyles, socioeconomic circumstances, and living arrangements of the inner city elderly.

The Urban Aged

In the past few decades the existence of geriatric ghettos in urban centers has become a subject of increasing national concern (Birren 1970; U.S. Senate 1978). Disproportionately high concentrations of elderly people are found in central cities compared with the suburbs (Golant 1975, 1979). In spite of losses from out-migration, the percentage of older people living in metropolitan areas actually increased between 1950 and 1975 because of the aging of the resident population (Lichter et al. 1981). High crime rates, inadequate housing, and the rapid expansion of urban renewal projects uprooting thousands of the aged from familiar neighborhoods where many have spent a good part of their lives all contribute to the problems of the urban elderly (Eckert 1979b). Forced relocation results in heightened grief, confusion, and isolation (Kasl 1972; Kastler et al. 1968); mortality may increase because of stress resulting from moves necessitated to make room for high-rise office buildings and expensive shopping centers. Thus the challenge confronting social planners is to assess the viability of inner city living given the survival needs of older residents and quality-of-life issues.

Statistically identified as one of the most deprived segments of the older population, the elderly living alone in the central city are typically viewed as suffering from extreme poverty, social isolation, and public neglect. At least part of the emphasis on the problematic character of city living for older people can be traced to the sociological writings of theorists who stressed the relation between the urban scene and alienated lifestyles. Rooted in the earlier work of Simmel (1950) and elaborated on in the writings of Zorbaugh (1926), Park and Burgess (1925), and Wirth (1938) is the view that the anonymity and complexity of urban living contribute to the breakdown of the intimate ties essential to human survival.[2]

Although more recent studies have questioned the validity of the urban-alienation thesis (Fischer 1973),[3] it has influenced studies of socially disadvantaged urban populations, as evidenced by the findings of several investigations into the social life of single, unattached elderly people inhabiting old hotels in the inner city. For example, Stephens (1976) depicted the older tenants of a deteriorating hotel in downtown Detroit as "loners" who, while displaying considerable survival skills were, nonetheless, social isolates involved in a zero-sum game for competitive survival. Lopata (1975) reached somewhat similar conclusions in her analysis of data derived from several studies of support systems among elderly urbanites in Chicago. Adopting a conceptual framework that assumed an essential lack of congruence between the needs and capacities of aged people on the one hand and urban conditions on the other, Lopata concluded that many elderly were unskilled in using the available community services and lived as social isolates or "urban villagers" in a world increasingly unresponsive to their needs.

Other investigations have documented widespread social and mental aberrations among the urban elderly, who are often indiscriminately included with drug addicts, alcoholics, and the mentally ill (Hertz and Hutheesing 1975; Isenberg 1972).[4] The portrait of the aged inner city dweller that emerges is, then, one of impotence, social failure, and an inability to cope with environmental demands. Research findings convincingly document the negative features of the inner city environment and how the lack of structural and social resources undermines chances for independent survival (Brice 1970; Rosenberg 1968; Shapiro 1971; Tissue 1971). Indeed, many elderly are poor and suffer from severe health losses (Cantor and Mayer, 1976); others are caught in a downward spiral of increasing isolation as friends die and poverty or limited mobility constrain their capacity to use buses and obtain decent housing at affordable prices.

Other studies, however, indicate that isolated lifestyles and situational incompetence are not necessarily typical of the urban scene (Sokolovsky and Cohen 1981). While investigating the social arrangements among aged residents living in twelve hotels in downtown San Diego, researchers found that many had lived in the central city for years and demonstrated considerable skill in coping with problems of survival (Erickson and Eckert 1977). In another comprehensive study of the aged living in New York City, Cantor (1975) found that 61 percent felt the city was a good or fairly good place for older people to live and pointed out the importance of such features as the concentration of needed services, easy access to public transportation, and the availability of low-cost rentals. Other studies have shown that many are following preferred lifestyles in accordance with long-established patterns ranging from reclusiveness to high levels of social involvement and that many also demonstrate considerable resourcefulness in meeting daily needs (Cohen and Sokolovsky 1980; Eckert 1980).

Such findings highlight the importance of additional investigations to examine the varying lifestyles, preferences, and range of adaptive capacities among the inner city elderly. Therefore, one of the primary goals of my study was to examine the heterogeneity of survival strategies and living patterns among residents of the St. Regis in their efforts to preserve familiar ways of life in a demanding urban world.

Most older people view independence as one of their main goals in life (Kalish 1967) and will seek to preserve their autonomy in the face of overwhelming odds. Advanced age, however, entails either the expectation or the reality of declining ability to function independently and the need for more supportive surroundings (Lawton et al. 1980). For those who are financially solvent and involved in social networks, needed help is more obtainable, whereas for many of the urban elderly, poverty, living alone, and limited access to support systems make them vulnerable to institutional placement. Thus, one of the most difficult adaptive tasks faced by the latter group is coping with the transition to a more dependent status when failing eyesight, reduced mobility, and chronic illness undermine the capacity for self-care.

The psychic and social costs of premature dependency are high, both for the individual and the society that must bear the financial burden of support. Programs and services that prolong viable roles in the community are therefore profitable both for those facing limitations in functioning capacity and, ultimately, for the community that must pay for their care. Currently, in the development of community-based resources for the mentally and physically disabled, a frequently stated objective is to enable them to live independently in their own neighborhoods for as long as possible. Referred to as the "normalization principle" (Wolfenberger 1972), this concept recognizes the dehumanizing consequences of institutional placement and the need to provide supportive services that are least disruptive to accustomed lifestyles (Biklen 1979). For those elderly who prefer to remain in the inner city, the question then arises as to what programs and facilities are most effective in prolonging autonomous living in familiar surroundings. A second major goal of my investigation was, consequently, to assess how living in an age-segregated environment extends the capacity of residents to remain at home. Access to assistance and protection from criminal victimization proved to be major determinants.

A number of investigations have demonstrated that living arrangements in which sizable numbers of elderly people share the same living space increase the availability of supportive help when crises occur (Hochschild 1973; S.K. Johnson 1971; Rosow 1967; Ross 1977). Several studies have already investigated the quality of life experienced by single, aged inhabitants of SRO hotels and have revealed that in spite of substandard conditions, aged tenants in these structures are able to benefit from help provided informally by other residents and hotel staff (Eckert 1980; Shapiro 1971; Siegal 1978).

Along a continuum ranging from independent housing to total dependency in an institutional setting, age-segregated planned housing may already be functioning in an intermediary capacity as an effective deterrent to institutionalization for those who find available support systems in residential hotels and privately owned apartment buildings no longer adequate. Older residents in urban public housing are more likely to have lower incomes, a greater number of physical infirmities, and fewer support networks than elderly people in other kinds of residential sites (S. Sherman 1975a, 1975b). Of interest is Bild and Havighurst's (1976) finding that those living in public housing units in Chicago referred to their living arrangements as "the place of last resort"— an evaluation that suggests that living in public housing may be seen as an adaptive response to increased needs and a preferred alternative to more dependent surroundings.

In addition to assistance needs, one of the most important survival concerns among the inner city elderly is protection from criminal assault (Braungart et al. 1979). Crime in American cities is highest in inner city areas and decreases in relation to the distance from the center (U.S. Department of Justice 1976). For many of the urban elderly, being old and poor constitutes double jeopardy. Greater age results in diminishing capacity for self-protection, and limited financial resources constrain them from moving to more expensive apartments and hotels where improved security features are expected in return for higher rents. Those in greatest need are thus often the most vulnerable.

Although public housing is frequently situated on the periphery of urban ghettos in areas of high crime and transient populations, several studies have indicated that residents in age-segregated housing experience lower rates of victimization and evidence less fear of crime than those elderly living in age-integrated facilities (E. Sherman et al. 1975). Understandably, older people are less likely to be preyed upon by their age peers, and the security features in public housing are generally superior to those usually provided in commercially owned, low-rental accommodations.

The St. Regis represents a unique type of residential facility that combines the autonomous character of SRO living with the greater protectiveness of planned housing. Compared with other public housing complexes and SRO hotels, which usually include families and younger tenants, the St. Regis has all elderly residents who live alone in self-contained apartment units. Tenants are generally expected to be self-sufficient in daily living, yet subsidized rentals, security guards, and the presence of a few concerned staff members provide more protection from outside dangers and the exigencies of advanced age than is usually found in privately owned units. Thus, in the pages that follow, I analyze the ways that living singly with age peers in the relatively sheltered surroundings of a public housing project affects the capacity for independent survival.

To what extent do similarities in age and circumstances influence the development of natural helping networks that can effectively supplement deficits in on-site services and local community resources? What degree of overall protection from both human and nonhuman threats in the urban environment is afforded by facilities of this kind? Does residence in this structure make possible the continuance of meaningful and familiar lifestyles? Answers to these and other questions will enable policy makers and official caregivers to evaluate the advantages and limitations of similar settings more effectively.

Last, my third major goal in this study was to examine the ways that the universal survival needs in later life transcend differences in socioeconomic status. Although the inner city aged are often particularly vulnerable because of poverty, substandard living conditions, and poor health, their fear of being alone in time of need, their preference for staying in familiar surroundings in spite of disabling illness, and their desire to remain independent are common problems of aging regardless of personal circumstances. Indeed, these concerns surpass age differences. Too often the aged in our society are viewed as a discrete group marked by problems unique to the old. Undeniably, advancing age increases the likelihood of declining capacities for independence, but viewing the problems of old age as separate and distinct from those of other age groups can only create barriers and instill fear of an age group we will eventually join. On the other hand, recognizing the commonality of basic human needs throughout the lifelong task of survival undermines these barriers and can lead to a more realistic appraisal of our own aging process.

In summary, much in the following pages is antithetical to generally held assumptions about the kind of life appropriate for the elderly. In assessing the suitability of the urban environment and the advantages of collective living in these surroundings, I have tried, however, to reflect the perspectives and concerns of those residing there (see Appendix, "In the Field"). Life in this particular community often involves hardship and despair when poverty and severe health loss threaten continued independence. Many structural features are not adequate for the extensive needs of the residents. Moreover, some tenants imperil their own well-being by refusing to obtain medical attention out of fear of hospitalization. But in spite of these difficulties, living with others in similar circumstances still seems to be an advantage in the task of independent survival.

Becoming Involved

My initial involvement in the St. Regis began in the winter months of 1975. One afternoon while visiting a multi-purpose senior citizens' center in another part of Los Angeles, I was introduced to a Housing Authority official who supervised a number of subsidized housing projects in the area I was interested in. When I described my research concerns and my wish to become involved as a volunteer offering counseling services, she suggested the St. Regis as a possible location. It housed approximately 245 single, elderly men and women. Funds were currently unavailable for counseling and recreational programs, and the needs of residents were extensive. I was, at the time, affiliated with a counseling organization that specialized in services for older adults. Through the use of trained volunteers, this agency had already established helping programs in another retirement residential hotel and wanted to extend their services to the downtown area. Thus I was in a position to offer the assistance of others in addition to myself.

Ten days later I was escorted around the St. Regis by a Housing Authority supervisor who was well acquainted with the building and its residents. We visited two apartment units occupied by women tenants who had been notified in advance that we would be dropping by. Both were well dressed and showed us around their small, nicely appointed rooms with considerable pride. Told of the reasons for my visit, they agreed that a counseling service was badly needed for the "sick ones." The site was ideal. The resident population was of manageable size, and the commuting distance from my home was reasonable. A small room was available for an office and would provide a quiet corner for interviewing and making notes. We agreed that I would come in two or three days a week and would be joined by additional counselors in several months.

After the visit, my guide spoke about some of the problems I could expect to encounter. In her opinion, many of those living in the building were mistrustful of outsiders offering help because of negative experiences with do-gooders and welfare agencies. Being accepted in this setting would depend on honesty, commitment, and patience in gaining trust and rapport. She described the residents as tough old-timers who had been on their own for a long time and who found it difficult to ask for help from anyone.

Thus began a commitment that lasted for two and a half years. During this time I became deeply and personally involved in the daily lives of people from whom I learned much about the vicissitudes of growing old.

Chapter 1

The Setting

On warm, sunny days a worn brick planter three doors away from the St. Regis is a favorite resting place for several of the elderly tenants. Mac,[1] a former Canadian who maintains he will never again "freeze [his] tail off in the north country," meets his friend Bill there almost every day after breakfast. As I stop to talk, Mac says he nevers gets bored sitting there. "Something's always happening," he remarks, waving his cane to an elderly woman who walks slowly by, carrying a bag full of groceries. "Living in my building is O.K. too," he continues, adding that it is a lot better than other places in the area. "I can't walk so good now and I need a place that's safe. I guess I'll stay here until they dig a hole and put me in the ground." His friend nods in agreement.

The St. Regis, where they both live, is a massive, nine-story structure in a transitional area adjacent to the central business district. A once prestigious hotel that catered to an exclusive clientele in the early 1920s, the building was reconverted in 1970 by the Housing Authority into a subsidized residential facility for approximately 245 single, elderly people of low income.

This action provided a partial solution to the housing needs of the urban poor, who were being uprooted by downtown redevelopment that replaced small stores, old churches, and housing dating from the turn of the century with towering office buildings and expensive hotels. An elaborate cultural center of several theaters, wide plazas, and graceful fountains now stands on a hill originally covered with old rooming houses and run-down apartment buildings. Some of the St. Regis tenants frequent a recently constructed shopping center within walking distance of the building. Although prices in the stores are generally beyond the reach of small pensions, the air-conditioned comfort of the inside mall provides a pleasant respite from enduring hot, smoggy days.

In a southeasterly direction one can see the characteristic signs of urban decay. Few residents will venture into "Skid Row" six blocks from the housing project. Although good prices can be found there, frequent muggings and robberies cause most of the elderly to do their shopping in more respectable parts of the downtown sector. Within a several-block radius there remains a number of apartment houses and hotels in obvious states of disrepair. Roaches are a constant problem and plumbing facilities are frequently inadequate. Occasionally one of these structures is condemned as unfit to live in, but people seem to continue doing so.

Directly across the street is the Stewart Hotel, which still retains an air of respectability. The restaurant on the ground floor is a popular eating place for nearby office workers. Clean, nicely furnished rooms are usually available, but recently increased rents caused several longtime residents to move across the street to the St. Regis. Next door is the James Hotel, which achieved some notoriety several years ago when an elderly occupant was murdered there by an unknown assailant. This building is badly run-down and has had several fires during the past year.

Occupants of these nearby hotels reflect the variegated racial composition of the downtown population. Young families recently arrived from Mexico, Asians, blacks of all ages, and elderly whites often share common living arrangements and regard each other with mutual suspicion. Recent influxes of Koreans and Vietnamese further complicate the population mixture, and Caucasian tenants at the St. Regis comment negatively about the increasing numbers of those who are different. In the words of one resident, "Too many Mexicans and coloreds are around these days. You can't even walk safely down the streets anymore." Elderly women residents express concern about the increasing numbers of old, black men.

One seventy-five-year-old tenant who has lived in the downtown district for fifteen years summarizes his feelings about inner city living in this way:

> The downtown area runs a higher percentage of senior citizens because of the conveniences—the things they need close by. And here you find mostly the handicapped person because of that same fact. In this area they have the conveniences of small stores, even though these small stores may take advantage of their handicap with high prices. And they are also close to the banks, which gives them an opportunity to get their checks cashed. And then they have the hotels —especially these public housing projects where subsidized rents make it possible for them to make the dollar go farther. But other hotels around here that operate without public subsidy—it's easy to see the difference. Some of these hotels are unfit to live in. One has been half burned and people are still living in it.
>
> And down here, too, the aged act as a very convenient pump. They pump social security money, vet compensation money, and SSI money into liquor stores and discount places. They keep these businesses alive. So that, after all, the senior citizen does serve a very important purpose.
> But at the same time he likes to believe that he's spending the leisurely part of his life in a first-class manner. And so he has nice parks to go to—with fountains that don't work— across from a hotel where suites cost three hundred dollars a night. And all this he gets to see by just a short walk.

Close to the St. Regis are numerous business establishments that cater to the daily needs of residents. Several markets, liquor stores, banks, drugstores, beauty shops, discount clothing stores, a post office, movie houses, restaurants, and a ballroom offer services and recreational opportunities at prices more in line with limited budgets. A locksmith charges sixty-five cents for duplicate keys; a cleaning establishment down the street launders shirts at prices below the rates in suburban areas, and a friendly clerk there calls many of his elderly customers by their first names.

In the barber shop next door, a sign in the window advertises discount prices for senior citizens, and the barber is known for his repertoire of jokes and his appreciation of good-looking women. Some restaurants in the area offer 15 percent discounts to senior citizens during off hours. But the small market just around the corner charges higher prices than larger supermarkets farther away. Those with limited mobility must pay these amounts unless a willing friend will bring back food bargains from more distant stores.

Across the street is Harriet's Cafe, where a hand-lettered sign advertises "Home Cooked Meals." This restaurant is a favorite gathering place for a group of women residents who go there regularly for brunch around eleven o'clock. A number of men prefer to go to Mason's Cafeteria, where a breakfast of two eggs, bacon, toast, and coffee can still be obtained for $1.50, and coffee refills are only 15¢. Some complain, though, that too many Mexicans work there now and the place isn't as clean as it used to be.

Two nearby churches provide a hot midday meal for sixty-five cents,[2] but few tenants take advantage of these inexpensive dinners. Most prefer to cook in their rooms or patronize nearby restaurants. One male resident volunteers to run the elevator at one of these churches in return for a free lunch. He likes to "help the old people out," although sometimes he finds himself becoming irritated by their constant complaining.

For days no longer structured by the regimen of work, the downtown area offers a variety of leisure activities. Nearby bars provide shadowy hideaways where, after the arrival of pension checks, serious drinking can be pursued in solitude. As early as eleven in the morning, several tenants can be seen perched on bar stools in Dino's Tavern just around the corner. For some, however, going out to drink is too expensive. A fifth of whisky purchased at the liquor store and consumed in the privacy of one's room is much cheaper.

The streets of this busy, crowded metropolitan area provide an unending parade of unusual events and characters. "Gutter Annie," an unwashed woman of undetermined age who dresses in cast-off clothing and pushes a baby carriage, can often be seen digging around for usuable refuse in city trash bins. One woman tenant says it's a shame that a person like that has nowhere to go. Traffic accidents are also noteworthy events. Says one resident, "I saw it all. This black kid—he missed the turn and drove his car right over the curb into the parking lot. A couple of people walking along, minding their own business, just managed to get out of the way in time."

Walking around is another favored way to spend time, although this activity is limited to the daylight hours because of safety concerns. One man, who gets up at five o'clock every morning, walks a minimum of fifteen blocks before breakfast. Another prefers to go on foot to the Central Market about a mile away to buy groceries at low prices. Moving about on the streets of the city provides a feeling of continuing participation in the outside world. Passersby consist of young Hispanic women with small children in tow, well-dressed businessmen on their way to lunch, housewives from the suburbs taking advantage of downtown sales, and young office workers dressed in the latest fashions. Being on the sidewalks near the St. Regis provides a fleeting association with others who are different, which assumes importance when one lives in a place where all are old.

Walking about also involves danger. One white-haired woman who moves slowly with the aid of a cane goes out several times a week to nearby department stores and the bank. "It's my only form of exercise, but I'm a sitting duck for purse snatchers." Many avoid the streets after dark, preferring to remain behind the safety of locked doors in a building where the presence of a security guard adds to the feeling of safety.

The St. Regis

Before its reconversion, the St. Regis was occupied by elderly retirees who were more or less permanent residents and by transient overnighters such as salesmen and Greyhound bus drivers. One woman resident who lived in the building at that time reminisced about the "good old days": "Before all these old people came, this used to be a good place to live. Then there was a bar, a good restaurant, and dances every Saturday night. But now all that is changed. Where the bar and restaurant used to be, got sold to outside people. Now the place is dead and just filled with a lot of gossipy old people."

Under the aegis of Section 23, a leased-housing program authorized by the Federal Housing Act of 1965, the hotel underwent extensive renovations in which small rooms were converted into larger, self-contained, single-occupancy units with cooking facilities and private bathrooms. Although still privately owned, the building is leased by the Housing Authority as a turnkey project in which units are sublet to eligible applicants who pay 25 percent of their monthly incomes for rent. Administrative details remain in the hands of the Housing Authority. To all intents and purposes, this agency functions as landlord and supervises the selection and rejection of applicants, collection of rents, and other personal details arising in the day-to-day operation of the facility. The private owners remain responsible for physical maintenance and are guaranteed the difference between rent paid by tenants and the fair market value as determined by comparable living alternatives in the area.

A large lobby and adjoining lounge occupy most of the ground floor (see Figure 1.1). Both areas are filled with comfortable armchairs and couches, but it is the main lobby that is the focal point of community life. The decor reflects a baroque style popular in earlier years. The high, vaulted ceiling is adorned with carved plaster borders; faded crimson-velvet drapes frame two bay windows that afford a wide view of the busy street. The somber wine carpet is worn in some areas but still retains a luxurious thickness that feels good to walk on. Recently the whole room was painted a bright yellow that somehow seems harsh in contrast with the faded furnishings. Four or five potted plants add a touch of greenery, and a large bulletin board by the elevators is covered with notices of senior citizen programs, Las Vegas tours, and nutrition sites. Any pictures on the walls have long since disappeared and have not been replaced. There is a widespread belief among tenants and staff that anything that isn't nailed down will be stolen. Mailboxes are located at the back of the room, and every day

FIGURE 1.1
FLOOR PLANS, ST. REGIS

4–9th floors

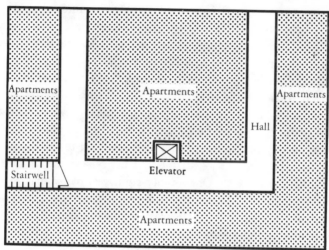

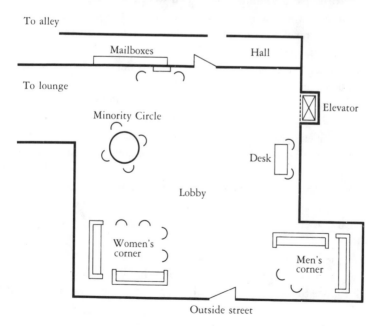

around noon at least twenty or thirty residents gather for the important daily ritual of picking up the mail.

The lobby also serves as the main route for entering and leaving the building. The front door is immediately accessible from the street, and there is no desk clerk to monitor the flow of passersby. Some of the lobby regulars voluntarily perform desk-clerking functions, however, and ask outsiders to sign a guest register kept on a large desk near the door.

Two occasionally unreliable elevators are situated toward the back of the lobby. Stories about breakdowns are a familiar part of community lore. Recently one man was stuck between floors for two hours before emergency repairs could be completed. "The poor old guy couldn't hold in his piss and had to let go against the wall," one tenant joked. Elevator use can also be a source of trouble in other ways. One seventy-eight-year-old woman relates how she refused to get on when an "old drunk" who lived down the hall confronted her. "He tried to put his hands on me and asked me to go back to his room for a beer. I told him to keep his filthy paws to himself and then went back to my own room. I didn't come out until I was sure he was gone." For others, elevator travel provides some enjoyable opportunities for sociable exchanges.

Jennie, one of the most attractive and popular women in the building got on the elevator to return a vacuum cleaner to the manager's office. Two elderly male fellow passengers perked up considerably at seeing her. She laughingly commented that her cleaning effort should last for at least six months. One of the men remarked that his place could "sure use a good cleaning." Jennie replied, "Well, I'm pretty expensive and charge ten dollars an hour." Knowing laughs were exchanged all around. As she got off on her floor she winked and added, "At those prices I don't get many takers." There was a warm feeling in the elevator after she had gone.

The second floor is rented out by the owners to a private business concern and has no connection with the residential sections. Entrance to this floor is possible only from an outside entrance on the east side and from a service elevator. The third floor is allocated to administrative offices and recreational areas. The Housing Authority offices are located here, away from main traffic patterns in the building. Residents often express concern about the necessity for outsiders inquiring into possible vacancies to go up to the third floor for information. Close by is the office for the Senior Citizens' Club, which is attractively furnished with a large desk and several comfortable chairs. A small library is next door. It contains several bookcases of well-worn paperbacks; an incomplete set of *National Geographic*; and an assortment of old, hardcover books ranging from poetry to biographies of famous people. One male resident voluntarily straightens up the shelves two or three times a week and complains about the disinclination of book users to put borrowed materials back where they belong.

Bingo games are held twice a week in a large recreation room at the end of the hall. The room is filled with long tables and chairs and has a seating capacity of approximately seventy-five. Adjacent to this room is a small kitchen with a sink, a small stove, and a refrigerator. The recreation room's decorations are sparse: an outdated calendar and several scenic photos from magazines are attached to the walls with Scotch tape. The walls are painted in an off-white, and the paint is cracked and peeling in a number of places. Some of the chairs need to be reupholstered, and the drapes are faded and worn. On Tuesdays and Thursdays several dozen women and a handful of men gather with the faithfulness of a devoted church congregation. Only half of the regular players live in the building; the rest come from nearby hotels and apartment buildings. Participants sit in their regular places, and conversation is minimal until refreshments are served by several women who live in the St. Regis. Usually, anyone who talks while numbers are being called is reprimanded.

A large, well-equipped poolroom is also located on the third floor. Games cost ten cents apiece, the money being used to make payments on a recently purchased new billiard table that is carefully covered with a heavy plastic cloth when not in use. Lighting is good. Several suggestive calendars on the walls contribute to

the distinctly masculine flavor of the room. At seven every evening, eight to ten men gather regularly for several hours of competitive play and a few surreptitious drinks. But it is the game itself, not friendship, that provides the focal point for interaction.
The "poolroom boys," as they are called by other tenants, do not
often sociably associate outside the poolroom.

Only a few women intrude upon this all-male activity. One
regular female participant, Josephine Wilson, who takes pride in
her pool-playing skills, is disdained by other, more respectable
women residents. Some suggest she is an "easy lay" who will
give a "blow job" to anyone who pays her ten dollars. Recently
Josephine broke her leg during an evening of pool. The circumstances leading up to the injury were never clearly known, but
stories that circulated often included the opinion that something
improper must have been going on.

Apartments are located on the fourth through ninth floors.
Each of the residential floors contains between thirty-five and
forty-two apartments that open into long, dimly lit halls. These
passageways are kept reasonably clean: the fading tweed carpet shows few stains and is regularly scrubbed; the walls were
recently painted a pale yellow. Burned-out bulbs are infrequently replaced, and the pervading gloom is not conducive to
sociable intercourse.

There is a boring uniformity to each of the floors, and floor
numbers in the elevator are hard to see. It is easy to get off on the
wrong floor and try to insert a key in a lock that doesn't fit. Residents say it is not unusual to wake up in the middle of the night
at the sound of someone mistakenly fumbling with one's door. A
few angry comments usually send the transgressor away. Those
few who routinely become confused about the location of their
apartments are viewed as becoming senile.

Apartments, rented fully furnished, vary in size. Each consists
of a medium-sized room containing a living and sleeping area,
a storage closet, and a partially separated kitchen with a four-
burner stove, oven, refrigerator, and work counter. All units have
fully equipped bathrooms with a tub or enclosed shower. The

Housing Authority supplies a bed, one armchair, a small eating table and chair, and a chest of drawers. Incoming tenants must supply their own bedding and linens and are usually not allowed to bring in large pieces of personal furniture. Suitcases and packing boxes have to be kept to a minimum because of the limited amount of storage space.

A number of apartments look singularly impersonal and reflect the solitary lifestyles of their occupants. George Miller, a quiet, gentle man who never married and is now in his late seventies, has lived in the same apartment for the past four years. A neatly made bed that doubles as a couch in the daytime is covered with a faded, tan bedspread carefully mended in several places. A black chair faces a small color TV set across the room. The plastic covering is a little sticky in places because he likes to sit there and eat dinner while watching news and sports. In the kitchen, aluminum foil is carefully placed around each burner on the electric stove. The small refrigerator, which is built in under the counter, contains some butter, half a quart of milk, and part of a meat loaf that can be made to last for another two meals. Several unwashed dishes are neatly piled in the sink; the drainboard and top of the small eating table are wiped clean. Two suits carefully covered with plastic laundry bags are hanging in the closet. A worn, plastic suitcase fills the top shelf.

The top of the old walnut bureau is devoid of any personal items such as photographs and souvenirs. There is only a black lacquered tray bought several years ago on a trip to Chinatown in San Francisco. On this tray are several shirt buttons and a needle and thread. No pictures hang on the walls. The only festive touch in the room is three paper flowers standing askew in a mayonnaise jar on the eating table. If George Miller should die, there would be little trouble dispersing his belongings.

Other units are more homelike, warm and cozy. Edith Smith's small apartment overflows with memorabilia and personal items gathered over the years. She has been living in the building for three years and, because of ill health, rarely leaves her room now except on necessary errands. But here she is surrounded by things she loves. The bed is covered with a brightly colored, hand-made quilt and accented by several pillows, each in the shape of an animal. Two small antique walnut tables that have been in her family are on either side of the bed, which doubles as a couch during the day. Photographs of herself as a young girl and of her husband, who died many years ago, occupy the bureau top along with such other knickknacks as ceramic animals and a grouping of tiny wooden elephants hand-carved in Taiwan. The walls are decorated with several felt hangings covered with pictures of birds and country scenes cut from magazines. She has also framed some Christmas cards received from friends in past years and attached them to the wall with thumbtacks.

Edith Smith is proud of her bathroom and happily shows it to any visitors. The hard lines of the toilet are softened by pink chenille covers, and a matching rug covers much of the old white tile floor. The small medicine cabinet is stuffed with an assortment of patent medicines, and the counter beside the washstand is littered with empty perfume bottles and cosmetics.

The kitchen area is well equipped and something is usually cooking on the stove. Pots and pans are hung on the wall, and a rack of spices is within easy reach. The refrigerator always seems too small and barely accommodates the stored food. Edith often gives some of her leftovers to a friendly man down the hall. She rarely eats out. Severe arthritis makes it difficult to walk to any restaurant, and she enjoys cooking for herself because it gives her something to do. Several English plates given her by a friend who died recently hang on the wall close to the small table where she eats most of her meals. A TV set and portable radio supply most of her entertainment, and she is a devoted follower of the soap operas.

The Staff

The regular Housing Authority staff is a manager, a receptionist, and several security guards. Maintenance personnel—a janitor, an electrician, and a part-time painter—are employed directly by the private owners. The small number of employees relative to the large resident population is a consequence of limited government funds and expectations of tenant self-care. In both structure and function, the St. Regis is formally designated an apartment complex of units designed for independent, self-contained living. Occupants are expected to tend to their daily needs, perform housekeeping tasks, and rely on their own resources when they need additional help. Informally, though, staff members provide many kinds of assistance that allow some tenants to retain residential status during periods of infirmity.

The manager is an attractive woman in her early thirties who, with her college background, has rapidly risen through the secretarial ranks of the Housing Authority to her present position. She works in the building three days a week and spends the rest of her time managing another public housing project close by. Between half past eight in the morning and half past four in the afternoon, a small but constant stream of tenants filters through her office with concerns ranging from complaints about noisy neighbors to requests for repairs of faulty plumbing. Her formal duties consist of interviewing and selecting new tenants, implementing Housing Authority policies, handling complaints, record keeping, and resident behavior control. Her disciplinary functions are well recognized and somewhat respected. As one woman says, "You can't get away with anything from her. She can be tough and knows how to put people in their place."

The receptionist is a sociable, friendly woman of sixty-five who works full time in the building. In addition to general clerical duties she is responsible for housekeeping inspections,[3] the initial handling of rental inquiries from outsiders, and operating the office when the manager isn't present. Residents often drop by for informal chats and personal advice. One man, for example, she instructed in the technique of applying a mustard plaster when he had a serious cold; another, she advised on how to pacify a recalcitrant girlfriend. Age similarities and a lack of official power contribute to the rapport she enjoys with many tenants. Complaints about neighbors and negative feelings toward administrative policies can be expressed to her in greater safety than to the manager.

Overall, management does not maintain a highly visible presence. Their offices on the third floor are somewhat isolated from the rest of the building, and there is no manager-in-residence during the night, on weekends, or on public holidays. An emergency number is provided, and the security guard is supposed to handle any situations arising during off hours. Tenants object to the unavailability of staff members during these times: "After all, they don't live here, and when they go home they don't have to think about what is happening to us." Some maintain that such apparent inefficiency is typical of anything operated by the government.

Currently, one security guard is on the premises at all times. In addition to providing protection, guards perform other services ranging from personal favors to acting in place of management when the office is closed. Officially, the guard patrols all public areas in the building, checking exit points and dealing with suspicious outsiders. He also investigates complaints about noisy neighbors, mediates disputes, and asks troublesome residents to refrain from offensive behavior (see Table 1.1).

Among the maintenance personnel the janitor (before his untimely death) was the one most closely involved in the everyday lives of residents. In his daily chores he was responsible for the cleanliness of public areas in the project. In return for a small fee, he was also available to individual tenants for general housecleaning chores such as shampooing rugs, washing walls, cleaning bathrooms, and scrubbing out stoves.

Tenant Selection and Eviction

Eligibility requirements state that applicants must have low incomes, live alone, and be at least sixty-two years of age. For example, in 1976 annual incomes could not be in excess of $6,175, and personal assets (real property, stocks, bonds, etc.) could not exceed $10,000. Some verification of income levels is required; yet in a few cases, fraudulent information has gone undetected. After one tenant died it was discovered that he had a bank account in excess of $80,000, and a successful claim was

TABLE 1.1

TENANT BEHAVIOR CONTROL

Complaints	Security guard actions
Harassment by unknown others:	
Attempts to open apartment doors	Investigation
Knocking on doors late at night	Investigation
Emptying ashtrays in front of apartment doors	Investigation
Disturbances by neighbors:	
Loud radios, TV sets	Investigation, reprimand
Loud talking, arguing	Investigation, reprimand
Noisy visitors	Investigation, reprimand
Knocking on walls	Investigation, reprimand
Verbal hostility:	
Insults, swearing	Investigation, reprimand
Disputes	Mediation, reprimand
Violence to others:	
Threatening gestures	Physical intervention, threat of arrest, report to management
Pushing, shoving	Reprimand, warning to cease
Stolen items	Investigation, recommendation to change locks
Disturbing behavior in public areas:	
Drunkenness, passing out	Reprimand, assistance to room
Urinating (in halls, lobby, elevator)	Investigation, report to management
Eating, drinking in lobby	Warning to cease
Careless behavior:	
Apartment doors left open	Reprimand, orders to close
Burning odors (food left on stove, smoking in bed, etc.)	Investigation, clearing floor if fire danger indicated
Leaving key in lock of apartment door, propping open exit doors	Removal, door locking, reprimand

SOURCE: Housing Authority Security Guard Reports 1976, 1977.

made against his estate for payment of back rent. Although management believes most tenants are truthful about their financial status, staff members are still alert for indications of possible affluence such as quality clothing, expensive vacations, and valuable jewelry. Accordingly, some residents are careful to hide costly articles and avoid mentioning expensive trips.

Prospective applicants are also assessed for their ability to care for themselves and for general demeanor. Slow movements, the use of a walker, and confused conversation are taken as indicative of declining competence, and applicants displaying these traits are encouraged to seek more protective surroundings. The manager also attempts to determine potential "troublemakers," a category that includes alcoholics, the mentally ill, those with intractable personalities, and transients. With such applicants management is often caught in a difficult dilemma. As a government agency they are entrusted with the responsibility of providing housing on a nondiscriminatory basis to those in need; on the other hand they are responsible for the safety and well-being of those already in residence. But as one Housing Authority official said to me, "Now if two people came in and there's only one room available—and one of them is a man who seems drunk and has a four-day beard and is dirty—and the other is a little old lady who is sweet and nice and appears clean—and both are equally eligible and in need—which one would you take?" Screening for behavioral problems can only be done superficially, however, for character references are not required, and accurate assessments of respectability and sociability are difficult to make during one interview. A number of those admitted turn out to be chronic alcoholics, and a few exhibit severe personality disorders.

Many residents are critical of admission procedures and feel management is only interested in whether applicants are able to pay the rent. Comparisons are frequent between the skid row character of newcomers and the "good old days" under a former manager remembered as more selective. Long-term residents are particularly vocal in this regard, often complaining that anyone can walk in off the streets and remain as long as he or she can pay.

Once residential status is granted, relocating tenants who become seriously impaired and evicting those who exhibit vituperative behavior is indeed difficult. Formal eviction procedures are cumbersome and time consuming. Legally, a tenant may be expelled for violations of lease provisions such as nonpayment of rent, fraud in reporting income, and poor housekeeping. Several notices must be sent to the offending person, who then has the right of appeal. These activities can, however, involve months of bureaucratic effort, so only two tenants have been formally evicted so far. In the manager's view, "We don't like to evict people. That's too complicated—it's easier to talk them out."

Generally management approaches problem tenants informally and uses verbal persuasion to convince them to go elsewhere. Behavior warranting the problem label is apt to be one or more of the following: excessive swearing in public areas, indecent exposure, visible alcoholism, inability to care for self, poor housekeeping, mental disorientation, vitriolic outbursts, threatening gestures, sexual advances, and failure to pay rent. The first stage in the talking-out process is a request for the offending tenant to come to the manager's office, where the manager issues a warning that the unwanted behavior must cease or the resident will be asked to leave. Usually these admonitions are effective, but sometimes repeated warnings are ignored; then the resident is again called to the office formally and requested to leave. In almost all instances these residents will leave without protest.

Tenants exhibiting increasing mental instability and those who become seriously ill can be among the most difficult to persuade to obtain more supportive surroundings. When the only alternatives are nursing homes and mental institutions, management's powers of persuasion are diminished. Obtaining proof of mental incompetence is a complex process, and impaired residents cannot be relocated without their personal consent. The following example illustrates how difficult these situations can become.

Jason Rogers, a small man of seventy-three, was almost totally confined to his bed. He continued to lose weight and suffered from severe gastric disturbances. A neighbor came in several times a day to bring him food and tidy his apartment. Staff members tried several times to persuade him to obtain medical help, but he angrily refused. Finally an emergency medical team was called, but he wouldn't let them in. In several weeks his condition became so serious that he finally allowed the security guard to call an ambulance. He was taken to the hospital, where he died a week later.

Overall, staff members show considerable leniency toward those who exhibit deviant behavior or become seriously ill. Many have nowhere else to go, and management sympathizes with their fears of institutionalization. The extent of this tolerance is reflected in the fact that those who had received the notation DNR (do not readmit) on their files when leaving had already been at the St. Regis for an average of 1.3 years. Levels of tolerance decline, however, in relation to the increasing visibility of severe physical decline and when nonconforming behavior becomes troublesome to others. In these situations staff and residents alike join in hastening the departure of those viewed as problems.

The Tenants

Population characteristics of the tenants are generally similar to those found in other studies of elderly urban groups (Bild and Havighurst 1976; Erickson and Eckert 1977) (see Table 1.2) but differ dramatically in certain features. For example, in most age-segregated settings, one will generally find more women than men, whereas in the St. Regis men outnumber the women by three to one.[4] Elderly women are less likely to live in central city areas. High crime rates, transient groups, poor living conditions, and large minority populations are not attractive features for the many women who have led more sheltered lives in traditional domestic roles. My own observations of the lifestyles of the women residents indicate, however, that many women who do live in these areas are true urbanites who possess the requisite skills to function effectively in these surroundings.

Unusual numbers of unattached elderly people are characteris-

TABLE 1.2
POPULATION CHARACTERISTICS OF RETIREMENT HOUSING SITES

Site	Number	Age (mean)	Race (percentage)	Male/female ratio (percentage)	Marital status (percentage never married)	Living alone (percentage)	Length of residence	Renter status (percentage)	Financial status
St. Regis, Los Angeles (1977)	243	74	White: 78 Black: 12 Other: 10	75/25	Men: 40.0 Women: 16.4	100	4.5 years (average)	100	Monthly average: $275
Working-class hotels, San Diego (1975)	34	66	White: 90[a] Other: 10[a]	97/3			3 years (average)	100	Monthly average: $266
Uptown residential hotels, Chicago (1975)	100	75.5	White: 97 Black: 3 Other: 0	47/53	Men: 23 Women: 20	88	38% < 1 year 27% < 5 years 34% > 5 years +	100	Median income: $245
Public housing, Chicago (1975)	100	76.4	White: 60 Black: 39 Other: 0	40/60	Men: 14 Women: 12	83	14% < 1 year 18% < 5 years 67% > 5 years +	100	Median income: $205

SOURCES: Bild and Havighurst 1976; Erickson and Eckert 1977.

[a]These figures represent racial divisions for the whole sample (N = 82), which included residents of skid row and middle-class hotels as well.

tically found in central cities, and the St. Regis inhabitants are no exception. Although the majority have been married at some point, 40 percent of the men and slightly more than 16 percent of the women have remained unmarried. Among those who were married, approximately 43 percent of the men and 69 percent of the women are widowed, and the rest are either separated or divorced (see Table 1.3).[5] Information was unfortunately not available to determine exactly how long previously married tenants have been widowed, divorced, or separated, but individual case histories indicate that significant numbers have been living alone for many years.

TABLE 1.3
MARITAL STATUS BY SEX, 1977

	Never married	Widowed	Separated	Divorced	Total
	% (N)	% (N)	% (N)	% (N)	% (N)
Men	40.0 (73)	42.8 (78)	8.7 (16)	8.2 (15)	99.7 (182)
Women	16.4 (10)	69.0 (42)	8.1 (5)	6.5 (4)	100.0 (61)
Men and women	34.2 (83)	49.3 (120)	8.6 (21)	7.8 (19)	99.9 (243)

In the St. Regis no tenant is currently employed on a regular basis. Many have stable work histories and have worked in skilled and semiskilled occupations for a number of years.[6] The men have been waiters, chefs, salesmen, carpenters, bellhops, railroad porters, electricians, construction workers, sheet metal workers, and seamen. One tenant searched for gold in the Sierras for ten years; another was a self-styled labor agitator who, while attempting to organize a group of agricultural workers in central California during the early 1930s, barely missed being lynched by a mob of angry ranchers. A few have been in the professions. One, for example, has a master's degree and headed a math department in a private boy's school for thirty-five years before retirement.

Although the majority of women were married at some point, many have not filled traditional domestic roles. Numbers have done clerical or service-oriented work for most of their productive years. Some were secretaries and bookkeepers; others were domestic workers and baby-sitters for private families. One was a sales-clerk in a downtown department store for fifteen years and only retired after a severe heart attack; another worked as a waitress and part-time cook in a downtown restaurant and retired at sixty-eight because of arthritic feet.

Almost all residents depend totally on old age benefits for support. In 1977, when federal poverty levels were established at $2,900 for single people aged sixty-five and over, annual incomes of the tenants ranged between $1,350 and $4,500. The average income was $3,300, and around 19 percent of the residents were below poverty guidelines. The financial position of the tenants is also comparable to that of many other elderly people in the downtown area, where poverty is the common correlate of the aging process. For example, in 1970, 24 percent of those aged sixty-five and over living in the downtown sector were below the poverty level (see Table 1.4).

For most tenants, social security, supplemental security income (SSI), and veterans benefits are the primary source of income, although some receive railroad retirement and civil service pensions in addition. Others have small savings accounts in which amounts ranging from several hundred to a few thousand dollars are allocated for funeral expenses or kept as protection against unexpected misfortunes. One man who deeply distrusted banks kept over one thousand dollars in a money belt securely fastened around his waist. When he was hospitalized shortly before his death, he insisted on taking this cash with him and the whole sum disappeared somewhere during the admission process.

In spite of limited incomes, a number of tenants express relative contentment with their small pension checks.[7] One man receives a total monthly allotment of $275 and states that he spends $69 on rent, between $90 and $100 on food, $30 on clothing, $20 to $30 on recreation, and the rest for items such as medicines, toiletries, and cigarettes. He sees little need for additional money and feels he is receiving what he is entitled to. In contrast, some women feel they can barely make ends meet. One comments she is only able to eat one meal a day and must buy her

TABLE 1.4
POPULATION CHARACTERISTICS OF ST. REGIS RESIDENTS
AND THE ELDERLY RESIDENTS OF DOWNTOWN LOS ANGELES

Site	Number	Race (percentage)	Male/female ratio (percentage)	Marital status (percentage never married)	Living alone (percentage)	Length of residence	Renter status (percentage)	Financial status	Income sources
St. Regis (1977)	243	White: 78.0 Black: 12.0 Other: 10.0	75/25	Men: 40.0 Women: 16.4	100.0	4.5 years (average	100.0	19% in poverty	Old age benefits: 99%
Elderly (65+) of downtown Los Angeles (1970)	1,925	White: 82.0 Black: 1.5 Other: 16.3	69/31	Men: 36.0 Women: 13.5	76.3	a	b	24% in poverty	Old age benefits: 80%
Elderly (65+) of downtown Los Angeles (1980)	2,511	White: 57.5 Black: 12.3 Other: 30.2	61/39					54.4c	

SOURCES: U.S. Bureau of the Census 1970; U.S. Bureau of the Census 1980.

aFor the downtown area, information is only available for senior renter couples. In 1970, 55 percent of senior couples in this area had lived in the same apartment from 2–5 years; 29 percent had lived in the same unit 6–10 years.

bInformation about renter status is only available for senior couples. Of this group, 90 percent of senior couples in the downtown area live in rented apartments.

cThis figure includes senior couples and single elderly.

clothes at a clothing stall in a church where used housedresses can be purchased for several dollars. Indeed such complaints are realistically based. Among eighty incoming residents in 1977, the average yearly income for women was approximately $200 less than that for men.

Aside from periodic cost-of-living increases in social security checks, there exists little chance of improvement. Attitudes of acceptance become effective coping mechanisms in situations promising little change. The ability to manage on these incomes is enhanced by subsidized rentals—residents were paying, on the average, around $65 a month for their rooms at the time of the study—but instances of hunger and material deprivation do occur. For some, the week before the arrival of monthly checks can be a difficult time of cutbacks in food, clothing, and medicine. Few, though, admit to these hardships. Being able to live within one's means seems to be a matter of personal pride in maintaining habits of thrift acquired in earlier years.

TABLE 1.5
RACIAL COMPOSITION BY SEX, 1970

	White % (N)	Black % (N)	Latin % (N)	Asiatic % (N)	Total % (N)
Male	62.0 (153)	5.7 (14)	1.6 (4)	1.6 (4)	70.9 (175)
Female	26.3 (65)	2.0 (5)	0.8 (2)	—	29.1 (72)
Total	88.3 (218)	7.7 (19)	2.4 (6)	1.6 (4)	100.0 (247)

While there has been some increase in the number of minority-group people living in the building, Caucasians have remained numerically dominant. In 1977 approximately 78 percent of the residents were white, 12 percent were black, and the rest were of Latino, Asiatic, native and American descent.[8] Between 1970 and 1977 the number of whites decreased by about 10 percent; blacks increased by approximately 4 percent; and there were slightly greater numbers of Latinos and Asiatics (see Tables 1.5 and 1.6). These variations reflect to some extent both the greater

TABLE 1.6

RACIAL COMPOSITION BY SEX, 1977

	White	Black	Native Indian	Latin	Asiatic	Total
	% (N)	% (N)	% (N)	% (N)	% (N)	% (N)
Male	56.8 (138)	10.6 (26)	0.4 (1)	4.1 (10)	2.9 (7)	74.8 (182)
Female	21.0 (51)	1.2 (3)	—	1.6 (4)	1.2 (3)	25.0 (61)
Total	77.8 (189)	11.8 (29)	0.4 (1)	5.7 (14)	4.1 (10)	99.8 (243)

influx of minority groups into the downtown area and Housing Authority efforts to achieve more representative proportions. These distributions are also somewhat comparable to racial divisions among elderly people in the central city as a whole. In 1970, for example, 82 percent of the inner city aged were white, 1.5 percent were black, and 16.3 percent were of other racial origins (Table 1.4).

Although chronological age alone is an unreliable predictor of levels of functional decline, a close correlation does exist between age and a number of pathological conditions (Lawton et al. 1980). These factors critically affect need for assistance and tendency to move into a housing environment where supportive help is more likely to be available.[9] Although the official age of admission at the St. Regis is 62, records show that in 1976 and 1977 the average age of incoming tenants was 70.5 years. This suggests that many prefer to live in privately owned and operated facilities until increasing age necessitates moving into more protective surroundings. Further, as Table 1.7 indicates, the mean age of residents living in the building in 1977 was 74, 128 were between the ages of 70 and 79, and 49 were aged 80 or more. The oldest resident was 97 and attributed his longevity to bourbon, good food, and women (in that order).

The advanced age of St. Regis tenants has important consequences for many features of community life. Instances of need for assistance are more numerous than in other settings, and illness and physical decline are more visible. A high percentage of the very old combined with the fact that the average length of

TABLE 1.7
AGE DISTRIBUTION, 1977

Age Interval	Number	Percentage of total population
55–59[a]	2	0.8
60–64	16	6.6
65–69	48	20.0
70–74	65	26.7
75–79	63	26.0
80–84	32	13.0
85–89	13	5.3
90–94	2	0.8
95–99	2	0.8
Total	243	100.0

NOTE: Mean age: 74.
[a]Although the official age of admission is 62, younger disabled persons are sometimes admitted under special circumstances.

TABLE 1.8
REASONS FOR VACATING

	Deaths[a]	Illness[b]	Manager's request	Other[c]	Total
1970	6	6	1	33	46
1971	11	14	2	32	59
1972	6	7	4	22	39
1973	16	9	—	16	41
1974	15	2	—	30	47
1975	13	4	—	23	40
1976	14	9	—	38	61
1977	16	8	2	26	52
Total	97	59	9	220	385

[a]From existing records it was not possible to determine if recorded deaths occurred in the St. Regis or after arrival at the hospital.
[b]Illness figures represent those who left the St. Regis to enter medical settings. The frequency is probably greater than indicated because some may have left and been admitted to hospitals or nursing homes without the knowledge of the Housing Authority.
[c]The term other includes those who left because of dissatisfaction, to live with family members, without notice, and for no known reason. It is also reasonable to assume that significant numbers in this group should be included in the "illness" category.

FIGURE 1.2
VACATING RATES, 1970–1977 ($N = 385$)

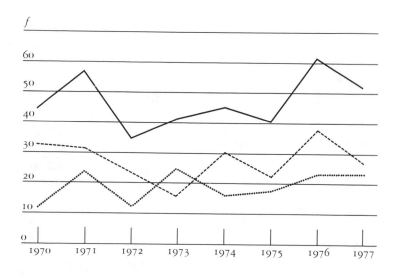

Key:

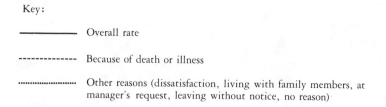

——————— Overall rate

------------ Because of death or illness

••••••••••••• Other reasons (dissatisfaction, living with family members, at manager's request, leaving without notice, no reason)

stay is 4.5 years should also result in increased rates of death and dying over the years; but as Figure 1.2 demonstrates, this has not necessarily occurred. Available records show that deaths and admissions to medical settings are understandably high and account for approximately 40 percent of tenants vacating since 1970. But between 1970 and 1977 these rates have shown no appreciable increase (see Table 1.8). In 1971, eleven persons died and fourteen were admitted to hospitals or convalescent homes; sixteen persons

TABLE 1.9
RATE OF VACATING

Year	Percentage
1970	18.7
1971	24.1
1972	16.0
1973	16.7
1974	19.1
1975	16.3
1976	24.8
1977	21.2

NOTE: Percentages are calculated using 245 as the average number of tenants each year between 1970 and 1977.

died in 1977 and eight were transferred to medical settings. The lack of increase is probably accounted for by the fact that incoming residents are considerably younger, which would counterbalance increased frequencies in death and illness as residents become older. These considerations should not, however, blur the reality that death and dying are prominent structural features in this community, where many are very old.

In similar fashion, overall vacating rates show little significant variation (see Figure 1.2). Since the community was first established, the average population turnover has been approximately 20 percent, with the range varying between 18.7 percent in 1970 and 21 percent in 1977. In 1971 and 1976 rates were, however, as high as 24 percent (see Table 1.9).

The picture that emerges is one of a retirement community that has shown considerable stability in residential patterns.[10] This stability has an important bearing on assistance patterns, safety concerns, and communal cohesion: Established helping networks are less likely to be disrupted. The ability to distinguish outsiders from those who legitimately belong is enhanced. In a setting where many avoid intimate ties, the continued presence of familiar faces provides at least some basis for a sense of togetherness.

Getting Acquainted

I began visiting the St. Regis on a regular basis just before Christmas in 1975. The manager suggested a festive coffee party in the main lobby around the time of mail delivery as an effective way for me to meet many tenants. Apprehensive about trying to break the ice alone, I enlisted the help of my seventy-five-year-old mother and two women friends who were experienced counselors. In making the plans, I neglected to provide any advance notice. When we suddenly appeared in the lobby around ten o'clock one rainy December morning carrying a large coffee pot, boxes of cookies, and a fancy tablecloth, some tenants evidenced surprise mingled with suspicion.

"What's this all about—what's going on?" one heavy-set woman exclaimed as we entered the front door. Somewhat awkwardly I explained that we were putting on a coffee party as a way of letting residents know about a counseling service that was going to be established with the permission of the Housing Authority. I added that, from then on, I would be coming on a regular basis to help out where I could. A woman standing nearby responded that it was about time they were getting someone like me in the building. "So many people around here need help, but most of them who live around here are only interested in themselves and their own affairs."

As we proceeded to set up the coffee pot and arrange refreshments on a large table, several tenants offered to help. One man even went to his apartment to get an extension cord so that we could heat the water. A man wearing a golfing hat and a brightly colored sports shirt came up to say that he and several of his buddies wanted to know what we were doing there. After I repeated my explanation and added that I was also interested in learning something about what living in the downtown area was like, he remarked that living there was just about the same as living anywhere else. "But I guess you're O.K.," he added and rejoined his friends in another part of the lobby. An attractively dressed woman observing our preparations commented on how nice it was that we would go to so much trouble to put on a party "for the poor folk." My heart sank as I realized how presumptuous it was not to have provided some kind of advance publicity and the patronizing way in which we had invaded their premises. How would I react if strangers appeared on the doorstep of my home with an offer to give a party?

During the next two hours we served coffee and cookies to approximately forty people, and in spite of an awkward beginning, a partylike atmosphere soon prevailed. Thanks to the considerable social skills of my mother and friends, our reception seemed favorable and most were having a good time.

While I was busily pouring coffee, I noticed my mother engaged in close conversation with an attractively dressed woman whose bright red hair stood out in sharp contrast to the more subdued coiffures of other women in the room. "Your mother shouldn't be talking to that person," a woman standing beside me remarked. "They call her Josephine and hardly any of us around here will have anything to do with her. She's one of the worst gossips in the place, and what we don't need around here are any more persons to spread bad stories. Too much gossip goes on already."

A short time later Josephine, the "troublemaker," came over to the refreshment table to get another cup of coffee. As we talked she told me something about her past life and her feelings about living in the St. Regis. She had been widowed for twelve years and came to Los Angeles from the East Coast six years ago because of the warmer climate. Most of this time she had lived in nearby hotels, and she finally came to the St. Regis a year ago when the place she had been living in was torn down. She liked the St. Regis because the rent was cheap and she was close to everything. But she didn't particularly like the other women. "They're jealous of my good figure [I could see that she was slim and well proportioned] and because a lot of men pay attention to me." She loved to go dancing and told me how she danced every dance a few weeks ago when she wore a black lace pants suit with flesh-colored undergarments. She often went to a ballroom several blocks down the street and met men there that she sometimes dated. "I don't have any trouble keeping my days filled—

there's usually something to do and time passes quickly. But I miss my husband, who died a long time ago, and no one will ever really take his place." Soon after this she left, saying she had a beauty appointment.

Henry Peters, a Caucasian man who appeared to be in his early seventies, came over and introduced himself. He was wearing a plaid jacket, well-pressed tan slacks, and a soft yellow sports shirt. When I explained the purpose of the party, he said he was glad "some of the people around here are going to get some help." He added that many were sick and pointed to an elderly black man who was slowly making his way across the lobby with the aid of a walker. "A man like that can't be expected to take care of himself properly, and yet they still let him stay here. He only manages because he pays several other tenants to help him out."

In response to a generalized description of my research aims, Henry made some observations about the ways in which the quality of residents had changed over the years: "When this place first opened up, people who lived here were a lot different. Then they had more get up and go. But in the last couple of years everything here has gone downhill. Most of the good ones either died or moved somewhere else. People coming in now just don't seem to care and don't want to do anything else but sit in the lobby all day." Few attended social gatherings that were occasionally held, and only eight or nine persons used to show up for weekly movies put on by a woman from the Department of Education. Because of his overall contempt for many who lived there, Henry spent little time in the building. "I just don't get involved with these people. I don't want them to know what I do during the day and so I keep to myself. I don't want them gossiping about my affairs."

At this point in our conversation Henry expressed a wish to help me get started and offered to introduce me to several residents he was on friendly terms with. "You'd find them to be much nicer than the ones who hang around the lobby," he added. He also suggested a good way to get to know people would be to visit them in their rooms. "A lot of the people here are loners and only like to talk in private." We made arrangements to meet again in several days.

As the party drew to a close, I felt much had been accomplished. During the morning I had met and spoken with at least a dozen people, and several had invited me to visit with them in their rooms. I had also obtained some overall impressions that differed considerably from the negative descriptions of the urban elderly I came across in my readings. Most I had met were nicely dressed, appeared to be in relatively good health, and said they were leading active lives. I realized that, to succeed with my study, I would have to discard preconceived notions and begin anew. Some of my own anxieties about entering a strange and unfamiliar setting were also alleviated. I was ready to begin.

Chapter 2

The Quality of Community Life

During my first few months at the St. Regis I was primarily involved in becoming acquainted with the residents and offering my counseling services as needed. The receptionist in the manager's office provided me with a list of several tenants who were ill and seemed to have no one to rely on. Soon much of my time was occupied with performing maintenance tasks such as food shopping, arranging for transportation to medical clinics, and writing letters for two men and one woman. Others were not as immediately receptive to my offers of help. A few who were similarly incapacitated politely told me they were being well cared for by families and friends. For instance, one woman I visited was recovering from a heart attack and had been confined to her bed for several weeks. When I asked if there was anything I could do, she abruptly replied that she was being taken care of by two neighbors and I "needn't trouble myself." As knowledge of my helping activities spread, though, trust and rapport grew, and direct requests for my assistance increased. Soon I became known as the "lady who helps the sick ones," and general interest in my research aims became insignificant in relation to the importance of actual services I was giving.

Through these activities I gained a deeper understanding of the difficulties faced by many tenants in their daily lives. I witnessed the frustrations involved in trying to locate missing social security checks and enlist the cooperation of harried public officials. I came to appreciate the fear many exhibited toward the possibility of confinement in convalescent homes and observed how often tenants left medical settings against their doctors' advice to return to their own apartments. I also found myself attempting to make sense out of complicated government forms and wondering how anyone could comprehend the obtuse language. And I learned how difficult even the simple acts of making a phone call or writing a letter can be when eyesight declines and arthritis sets in.

About half of my time I spent visiting residents in their own apartments. Sociable contacts were often a private affair, and many I talked with preferred the seclusion of their own rooms.[1] There were, however, many occasions of conversational exchange in public areas such as the lobby, halls, and elevators. I also spent time with residents in nearby restaurants, stores, medical clinics, and hospitals and walking around the city streets.

After three months, I was joined by other counselors, who spent a minimum of four hours a week in the building.[2] Together we set about establishing group activities such as a garden club, a discussion group, an arts and crafts class, movies, and a monthly coffee party. The weekly movies and the coffee parties we held in the main lobby on the day that social security checks arrived were most successful, measured by tenant participation. The most important kinds of assistance we provided were direct aid in locating missing pension checks and negotiating medical bills, referrals to community agencies and one-on-one visitation. Many residents, however, remained aloof, preferring to rely on their own resources and attend recreational and social activities on the outside.

Formal Organizational Features

In this early period I was struck by the abundant evidence of apparent social disorganization. Themes of apathy and noninvolvement in community activities prevailed in stories often repeated by staff and tenants alike. A Housing Authority official described to me how she attempted to establish a nutrition program in which meals were served several times a week in the recreation room on the third floor. But most tenants preferred to eat in outside restaurants or in the privacy of their own rooms. Poor attendance put an end to the service in a few months.

The Senior Citizens' Club was often described by residents as an ineffectual organization riddled by internal dissension and impotent in its efforts to influence the course of community affairs. Many did not attend its meetings held once a month in the lounge because they considered them boring. Others refused to accept official positions in the club because of the amount of public criticism directed at those who accepted leadership roles in the past. Several years ago the treasurer had resigned in disgust because of gossip that inferred she had stolen funds amounting to several hundred dollars. Elaine Michaels, an attractive, congenial woman in her late seventies, the current president, expressed a wish to resign because so few appreciated her efforts. The following description of a meeting that took place a year after I entered the setting illustrates the kinds of difficulties involved in promoting group activities among members of a population who appeared to be uninterested in and unfamiliar with the techniques of group process.

The main purpose of the gathering was to elect a new president. Mr. Turner, a representative from the Department of Parks and Recreation, was present to initiate the proceedings. The meeting was held in the lounge, and when I arrived, about forty people were already seated in chairs and couches arranged in long rows in front of the piano. I was surprised by the large turnout, but a man sitting next to me said people came only for the free doughnuts and coffee. Mr. Turner opened the meeting by stating that Mrs. Michaels wanted to resign, making it necessary to elect a new slate of officers. A man sitting in the front row suggested the name of Sara Ross. She was well known in the community and enjoyed a variable reputation as a gossip, a drunk, and a good friend. I turned around and noticed that Sara was sitting quietly in the back of the room. Her name immediately provoked loud guffaws. Someone called out that she was drunk all the time, and "who needs a drunk for a president?" Somewhat unsettled by this outburst, Mr. Turner then mentioned the name of Harry Redinger, who was popular with many residents and considered a good storyteller. A woman got up to say his name should be withdrawn because he wasn't there and she personally knew that he wasn't interested in the job. Several other names were suggested, and each time there were objections from the group. Side discussions started in which people began arguing over whether or not Elaine really wanted to resign.

Mr. Turner was becoming angry. No one seemed to be paying attention and he was losing control. In frustrated tones he asked if anyone wanted to volunteer. There was no response. "Now how can I help you if you don't want to help yourselves? It looks to me like you people don't want a club." I found myself thinking that his attitude was contributing to the general disorder now beginning to prevail. Ignoring the rules of parliamentary procedure, he then tried to have a vote for Sara Ross. Six people held up their hands in support of the nomination and about ten people voted against her. Mr. Turner then exclaimed, "Now how can it be that only fifteen people voted when there are about forty of you sitting in the room? Are there any people who will volunteer?" There was no response, and some man commented that they might as well try to nominate the "Shadow." Mr. Turner again asked if they wanted to get a club started. A man standing by the entrance said, "What club?" Laughter and joking followed. People began to disperse and broke up into small groups around a table that was laden with coffee and doughnuts.

The man sitting next to me described how a couple of years ago he tried to get a dance club started but only a few showed up. "Trouble with the people around here is that they are nine-tenths dead. They never want to do anything," he added. He did express some surprise that the meeting had broken up so quickly. "But what can you expect when they nominate a drunk for president. This kind of thing goes on all the time." He got up and went over to get some coffee.

Several months after this meeting there was an effort to obtain more club members who lived on the outside. An energetic woman who lived in a hotel several blocks down the street was persuaded to accept the office of president. Under her leadership the club has regained some vitality, although only half of the members are St. Regis tenants. Current activities include a bi-weekly bingo game held on the third floor and occasional recreational outings held in conjunction with other senior citizens' clubs in the area.[3] One of the most popular events is a tour to Las Vegas every three or four months. Around a dozen residents regularly travel on buses for three days and nights of revelry and gambling at reduced rates. On one trip a tenant married a woman he had been engaged to for several months, and champagne flowed freely on the return journey.

In contrast to the Senior Citizens' Club meetings, programs dealing with survival concerns are well attended. For example, every month the police show films and give talks on pertinent safety topics such as self-defense and reducing exposure to criminal victimization. Forty to fifty residents regularly participate and listen attentively. At one meeting a police officer sold whistles for fifty cents each and gave the following instructions on their use: "Now really blow hard if you're in danger. It's a good way of attracting attention and getting help. When you're alone and out on the streets, you should carry your keys in your hand and have the whistle attached to a key ring or else wear it around your neck."

He went on with advice about carrying money. "Now what do some of you do when you have to carry funds?" One amply endowed tenant jokingly put in that she carried her money in her bra. "They'd have trouble finding it in there," she added, indicating the size of her bosom, prompting considerable laughter. "Carrying your money close to your body is good idea," the officer responded. "But never carry more than you absolutely need, and you shouldn't even carry a purse unless you have to. The police can't be everywhere all the time, so you have to be careful and look out for yourselves."

The officer then cited the problems of limited funds for adequate police surveillance and the reality of high crime rates in the downtown area. Stressing that it was impossible for the police to provide adequate coverage, he stated that assistance was really only available in emergencies and for truly serious crimes. Self-help and knowing how to behave in careful ways were the keys to making it in the central city. As the meeting broke up, resi-

dents filing out of the room made around two dozen police whistles purchases.

The frequent lack of participation in planned activities is affected by three salient conditions: independent lifestyles characterized by limited organizational experience, concerns for privacy
in daily affairs, and administrative procedures restricting tenant
participation in decision making affecting community life. Some
women and a few men belong to charitable societies and participate in union activities for retired members. Elaine Michaels, for
instance, speaks with pride about her former positions of leadership in community organizations, and Gregory Roberts, a former
jazz musician, regularly attends meetings of the Musicians Union
and volunteers to raise funds for the Epileptic Society. But as
Mrs. Michaels said one day in my office; "These meetings of the
Senior Citizens' Club are hard to conduct. Most of the people
who go don't seem to know how to act. Everybody talks out of
turn, and they don't even know how you take a vote." For many,
working-class backgrounds and years of marginal subsistence
have not been conducive to the development of a middle-class
perspective on the virtues of charitable work and membership in
community groups.

Other residents say they are reluctant to become involved because they prefer to limit their contacts with other tenants and to
maintain secrecy about their personal affairs. When I asked one
woman about her reasons for attending bingo games at a church
several blocks away, she replied: "Almost everyone who goes to
this church is from somewhere else. You go there, you have your
good time, and then you leave. Because everybody is from somewhere else, there can't be much backbiting or gossip. Trouble is
that when you live in a place like this, everybody knows everybody else and knows what everybody does. That's why a lot of
people do things in other places. Because we all live together
—that doesn't mean we have to do things together. There's less
trouble that way." On numerous occasions I heard similar opinions from others. For these residents, nonparticipation in on-site
events becomes an effective mode of adjustment to the circumstances of group living and enables the continuation of privacy in
ways that are congruent with long-established patterns.[4]

Last, the lack of tenant involvement is influenced by feelings of being powerless to influence administrative policies. In structure and function, the St. Regis is a "centrally administered community," which is defined by Fry (1979) as a locality in which power and control are concentrated in the hands of a few designated officials. This mode stands in contrast to that of a "corporately administered community" in which members are more actively involved, through voluntary associations and elected bodies, in decision making and management functions. The administrative staff at the St. Regis occupies a position of unquestioned authority in the execution of major policies affecting many sectors of community life. Tenant selection and eviction processes are determined according to official rules of residence, although the right of appeal exists. Unlike tenants of other public housing developments (Francis 1981; Kandel and Heider 1979), St. Regis tenants have few opportunities to influence administrative policies through elected bodies such as a tenants' council.[5] Group efforts to achieve change are short lived, and some residents say they will not become involved for fear of being labeled troublemakers. On one occasion several women tried to obtain signatures on a petition to increase the number of security guards, but few would consent to sign. Channels of communication are limited to individual confrontations in the manager's office when problems arise. In spite of many acts of kindness, the dominant administrative attitude of one of benevolent paternalism.

All this does not mean, however, that efforts to organize activities in this and similar settings are not worthwhile. In spite of limited membership, the Senior Citizens' Club sponsors a number of activities such as the bingo games and out-of-town tours that are appreciated by the participants. Management efforts to open avenues for tenant inclusion in administrative decisions through either the Senior Citizens' Club or a tenants' council could perhaps persuade some who possess leadership skills to accept official roles in policy-making committees. Given the widespread interest in survival concerns evident from the success of events sponsored by the police department, programs offering vital information on topics such as social security benefits and Medicare/Medi-Cal benefits are likely to be well received. Activities and events congruent with the perceived needs and sociability preferences of the recipients can be expected to have the greatest chance of success in settings of this kind.

The Patterning of Social Relationships

Although many tenants remain aloof from participation in formally organized activities within the building, a number of informal subgroupings exist that provide distinguishable internal borders marking roles and identifiable statuses among the residents. Many of the social cliques that define the tenuous infrastructure of community life are located in the large central lobby that functions as a social marketplace. It is here that significant community happenings such as the arrival of mail and the passing parade of those entering and leaving the building occur. Important communication processes are also in operation. Reputations are made and broken; judgments about the character and likeability of new tenants are formed; and information about suspected love affairs, deaths, and quarrels between neighbors are carefully dissected and analyzed. Describing the flow of events in this area thus becomes a way of viewing the social organization of a collectivity where ties between members are limited at best.

As early as seven in the morning several members of one regular grouping begin to congregate to discuss the newspaper headlines and yesterday's winners at the track. Well-known and influential, this gathering of a half dozen men and several women is referred to as the "Minority Circle," a label derived from the fact that participants represent a mixture of racial backgrounds and habitually gather around a circular coffee table in the center of the lobby. Conversation is usually lively and focuses on sports, the weather, politics, and newsworthy events about other residents.

One woman, whose name was romantically linked with one of her neighbors, commented angrily about the way this group spread falsehoods about their relationship: "Things happen, but in the telling, the good parts are forgotten and the bad parts remain. If the story is dull it gets added to, so that in the end, there's no way you can recognize the original thing that happened. I went out to dinner once with this nice old man who lives down the hall, and those old fogies in the lobby had us eloping to Seattle."

The recognized leader of this group is Charles Mason, an impeccably dressed and handsome black man who is found sitting in his favorite chair from early in the morning until late afternoon. One tenant comments that there are two things in life he can be sure of: "taxes and that old guy sitting staring at me every morning when I get off the elevator to go out to breakfast." Reactions to him vary from contempt to respect and liking. From the viewpoint of those who pursue a busy life on the outside, he is a nosy gossip who epitomizes the uselessness of old age. One black woman expresses fear that he will cause trouble for her by spreading malicious gossip because she resisted his advances: "That kind of person gets a feeling of pleasure out of being able to manipulate other people and being able to control them. And the danger is that when you don't do as he wants, he'll turn on you."

In contrast, Betty Hawkins, a congenial woman who is a regular member of the circle, speaks of him with admiration. He recently loaned her some money until her pension check arrived, and she describes how he often visits other tenants in the hospital when he feels they might be lonely. But regardless of these varying judgments, there is little doubt that Mr. Mason is one of the most dominant figures in community life, whom even management grudgingly recognizes with the label "influential troublemaker."

Other Minority Circle members are people who, for a variety of reason, are also well known. For example, Jennifer Williams is considered the most attractive woman in the building. Her youthful face and slim figure cause many heads to turn as she walks by. Roy Wilkins, a tall, spare man in his late sixties, is her regular companion and usually sits beside her. Their close relationship prompts considerable speculation as to whether they are sexually involved, but recent rumors imply that Jennifer is also dating men on the outside. Another participant is Henry Booth, a tall black man whose affable personality and penchant for storytelling make him popular and well liked. Mrs. Ling, a tiny Oriental woman who was an elementary school teacher before retirement, is also a regular member; she feels she has little in common with many tenants because of her education and professional background. Clearly this group occupies an elite status and is viewed by others as snobbish and condescending in their clannishness and disinclination to associate with others.

Later in the morning an all-male grouping of six to eight tenants begins to gather in a part of the lobby known as the "men's corner." Here, conversation is sporadic, and regulars will sit reading the newspaper, staring out the window, or falling asleep. Bob Sawyer, an unmarried retired electrician in his mid-seventies, usually sits in a chair close to the window and remains engrossed in the sports section as the morning hours slowly pass. Only occasionally does he exchange a few comments on the weather or baseball scores with George Kennedy, a former restaurant worker who sits on the far end of the couch watching tenants pass by. An aura of negativism is attached to this clique, and some residents refer to them as the "Hate Group." New tenants who mistakenly wander into their territory quickly respond to the gaze of unfriendly eyes and depart. Some women are particularly annoyed, for they feel they are being mentally undressed as they walk by.

Shortly before noon, members of a group known as "The Girls" come in from a late breakfast at Harriet's Cafe and wait for the arrival of the mailman in the area of the lobby known as the "women's corner." Five women constitute the core membership and are noticeably similar in their makeup and dress. Aged faces are brightened by rouge and frosted lipsticks; hair is carefully arranged; and clothes are fashionable and colorful. These women regard one another as close friends and frequently exchange help during illness. Elaine Michaels, the president of the Senior Citizens' Club, is clearly the leader, and her attention is coveted by the others. She describes how she was able to return from the hospital and avoid recuperation in a convalescent home because two of the women, Jean and Ruby, did her shopping and prepared her meals. "Without both of you," she says, leaning over and patting Jean affectionately on the knee, "I probably wouldn't have been able to make it back." One woman in this clique occupies a borderline position. She is known to drink heavily and during her binges will become quarrelsome and use abusive language. When this happens, other members refuse to talk to her, and she will defiantly sit in the men's corner while waiting for her mail.

Other residents occupying a marginal status in the tenant population, because of personal preference or disagreeable reputations, usually will sit in two locations that provide at least some sense of participation in the ongoing scene. Several come down an hour before mail delivery and sit in chairs around a large, old-fashioned desk next to the elevators. Anne Baker, a Caucasian woman regarded as one of the most disagreeable residents in the building, can often be found there at noon playing solitaire. Frequently she looks up to scutinize anyone passing, but few speak to her because her remarks are often sarcastic and insulting. George Livingston, an aged black man with a heart condition, usually sits in a chair on the other side. His appearance now is unkempt because of his declining ability to take care of himself. Some complain they don't like to get near him because of his body odor; others say he should at least get someone to cut his fingernails. "He can't control himself any more, and I even saw him relieving himself in the lounge the other day when he thought nobody was looking," says one woman. But sitting in his favorite chair and nodding his head in recognition to others constitutes an important form of social involvement and occupies several hours in a long, unchanging day. Before his stroke, George was rarely found in the lobby and preferred to spend his time riding buses to outlying areas of the city. Now his social world is confined to the lobby, which is better than remaining in his room.

The other area frequented by marginal members is a table and two chairs next to the mailboxes. The location guarantees at least some limited interaction with others as they come to pick up their mail. Several men and one woman can generally be found there around noon. Lucille, a reserved and quiet woman in her middle seventies, says she doesn't like to talk very much with people who sit in the lobby because of the bad gossip that goes on. Still coming down and sitting at the table is a way of passing time, and she can at least exchange minimal greetings with some people without getting involved in lengthy conversations.

Some reclusive tenants seek the privacy of the lounge, a large, cavernous room connected to the main lobby by a short passageway. In spite of a piano, armchairs, and couches, the limited lighting and isolated location create an atmosphere of gloom. Some call this room the "inner sanctum," and a story is often repeated about a woman who had her purse stolen while sitting in there. For a few tenants who purposely avoid associating with others, the lounge offers a quiet refuge from the busy hubbub of the lobby scene. An elderly man who is totally deaf prefers this room because he feels others in the lobby make fun of his attempts to communicate. Maria Lopez, a tiny Mexican woman who speaks only limited English, sits in there and reads magazines written in Spanish; an eighty-year-old man with a thick German accent expresses contempt for the "lobby lizards" and sits in the lounge so he "can keep away from those useless people."

By one o'clock, around thirty people are often in the lobby, and an air of excitment prevails as someone notes the mailman is approaching. One tenant comments on the importance of the event in this way: "Now some of these people around here—they hardly get any mail but they come down anyway. But then a lot of them don't have anything better to do."

The mailman arrives. He is young, black, and relatively new on the job. He has been criticized for getting the mail mixed up, and some claim he is practically blind. He doesn't greet anyone and goes unsmilingly about his business. There are four main sections of mailboxes, each containing sixty-two slots that are numbered according to the tenants' rooms. It takes the mailman about five minutes to place the mail in each section, after which he locks the partition doors in place. It is an understood rule that all should wait until the mail is distributed before attempting to retrieve their letters. Each tenant has a small key for this purpose.

One man pushes his way through and starts opening his box before the mailman is finished. Another woman who has been patiently waiting tells him to get back where he belongs and take his turn like everyone else. In response to his "bugger off," she retreats in anger. He then takes out a lone envelope and goes directly up to his apartment without speaking to anyone. Finally the mailman finishes, and the activity becomes more intense. A few push and shove but most wait politely. An elderly woman manages to catch the mailman before he leaves and demands to know if he put her social security check in the wrong box. He says he doesn't know anything about it and quickly escapes out the front door. One resident wryly remarks, "That poor guy. He makes this the last stop on his route. After he's finished here he's really had it. He only makes it about four out of five trips. The last time he gets an extra to do it."

After this important ritual is completed, the crowd begins to thin out. Some go back to their rooms for a midday snack followed by a nap; others leave for the bank or go food shopping; a number remain in their usual places, reading, chatting, or just sitting, for the rest of the afternoon.

The arrival of an ambulance and the sight of attendants maneuvering a stretcher through the lobby is not unusual at some point during the day. There is no other way for a medical unit to enter the building, and one man comments that "they come and go like that at least two or three times a week." It's three o'clock in the afternoon, and an ambulance pulls up to the front door. "I wonder who they're taking away this time?" one woman quietly remarks. The attendants enter the building, pushing a stretcher, and take the elevator upstairs. In about ten minutes a loud alarm begins to ring; someone remarks that the "damned elevator is stuck again." Conversation turns to the frequency with which the elevator breaks down and "why don't these Housing Authority people fix things properly." No one seems concerned about the possibilty that the ambulance crew might be stuck between floors with someone in need of medical attention. Fifteen minutes later the electrician has made the needed adjustments and the elevator finally comes down. The two attendants emerge with a man wearing an oxygen mask lying on the stretcher. The worried electrician receives reassurance from the medical team that their charge is all right. They go quickly through the lobby to the waiting ambulance outside. Within fifteen or twenty minutes, the ailing tenant will be receiving needed medical care.

Conversation continues on the apparently more newsworthy

event of the elevator being out of order again. Then Charles Mason asks a man sitting beside him if he knows who the man was who had just been taken away. His friend replies that he thinks it is "some guy who's been around for a couple of years, but no one hardly ever saw him because he always stayed in his room." I am sitting in the Minority Circle at the time and ask a woman beside me if residents find the frequent appearance of an ambulance upsetting; she responds, "Well, yes, in a way. You see, you never know if it's going to be your turn next."

Around five o'clock the front door is locked by the security guard—a procedure some lobby regulars jokingly refer to as "lock-up time." Most of the chairs and couches are empty now as residents leave to eat dinner in nearby favorite restaurants or to prepare a meal in their own rooms. Those who eat out like to go early so they can be assured of returning before dark, the streets at night being dangerous.

By eight o'clock a different group of tenants comes down for an hour or two of sociable conversation before going to bed. One regular grouping of three men and two women customarily meets in the same area used by the Minority Circle during the day. Other tenants jokingly refer to this gathering as the "Knights of the Round Table." Beatrice and Isaac, a well known couple in the community, are the focal personalities and dominate much of the interaction. For an hour or two, members will sit talking and laughing about the events of the day until someone suggests going up to an apartment for some coffee.

The lights in the lobby are left on all night for security. Taking advantage of this circumstance, another group of three or four men and several women who have difficulty sleeping come together with such regularity that they are known as the "Night People." Often their nocturnal visiting lasts until four or five in the morning. John Barrington, a congenial black man who has lived in the building for three years, describes his reasons for being there in this way: "Sometimes I go down just to be able to get out of my room and talk to people. Quite a few of us go down, and we're different than the ones who sit there in the day. Sometimes we sit and play the piano and sing; sometimes we just talk and laugh it up. Lots of times I can't sleep and going to the lobby is a lot better."

Being in the lobby late at night can also be interesting in other ways. Around half past eleven several women return from Marvin's Ballroom just down the street. On the way home they have stopped for a couple of drinks and are now laughing together about their experiences of the evening. Marjorie, an attractive woman who rarely admits to her seventy-five years, says she didn't sit out one dance. Clara Barstow, a black woman in her early seventies, is sitting by the front door and remarks to a woman beside her about how stupid it is for these ladies to be out by themselves so late at night. "They could be raped and robbed," she adds. Her companion, who is on the verge of falling asleep, nods drowsily in agreement.

About an hour later a young woman dressed in a tight blouse and skirt rings one of the outside doorbells connected to a tenant's room. Several residents sitting in the lobby start laughing and wonder who will be coming down to let her in. A few minutes later a male tenant appears and the two disappear upstairs. Someone comments that he doesn't think the visitor is the old guy's niece. Around two in the morning a disheveled looking woman kicks and bangs on the securely locked front door, yelling that she wants to come in and watch TV. She is quickly recognized as a nonresident, and Clara angrily tells her to go away or they'll call the police. Muttering a few obscenities, the woman disappears in the dark.

Those who sit and talk during the long hours of the night are tolerant of a few who just come down and fall asleep on one of the couches, but some residents who prefer to stay in their rooms at night can react angrily to the activities of the Night People. One woman locks her apartment door by six o'clock every night and observes that those who sit in the lobby so late at night should be kicked out. "Why don't people like that go to bed when they're supposed to? I do."

By four or five, most have gone to bed and the lobby is briefly empty. But at five-thirty sharp, with the regularity of clockwork, the elevator doors open and Charles Mason appears, neatly dressed and ready for his morning walk of fiteen blocks before breakfast.

Intratenant Relations

Although the lobby interaction I have described demonstrates sociable cliques and warm ties among some residents, the norm is distance rather than closeness. The comments of Ted Robinson, a long-term resident, are typical of tenants' opinions about the dubious character of others living in the building: "The people around here don't know right from wrong and they'll take anything that's left lying around. They have no sense of respect for other people's property. This one guy came into the lobby with a bag full of groceries and sitting on top was this big roast. He just put the bag down for a couple of minutes while he went to pick up his mail and when he came back the roast was gone. But that kind of thing you can expect from the people around here."

Issues Affecting Tenant Interaction

Although theft and physical harassment happen rarely, stories of such events are frequently told as proof of the questionable character of some tenants. For instance, Clara Barstow's version of a fight that happened six months after I was in the building is one of the most often repeated examples of the kind of violence that one can expect:

> This fight that happened just shows you how people treat each other around here. The one who attacked this other guy—he used to be nice but lately he'd gotten to acting crazy and saying mean things. He got on the elevator with Jim, who is the kind of guy who wouldn't give anybody any trouble—and made some crack about the Dodgers. I don't know exactly how the fight got started, but he knocked Jim down and the bag of groceries he was carrying spilled all over the floor. Anyway, this crazy guy was beating him up, but the janitor came by and pulled him off. And awhile back this same guy threatened to hit some woman over the head

with an ash tray. People like that are dangerous to have around. You can never tell what they are going to do.

In reality actual violence between tenants is rare. While I was in the setting I was only aware of one or two other incidents in which tenants attempted to inflict bodily injury. Verbal threats do occur at times, and their frequent recounting increases public apprehension. Fears are compounded by the belief that dangerous people are hard to get rid of once they are in the building.

Some women have been victims of practical jokes. Mrs. Melton, a seventy-six-year-old tenant who constantly complains about the character of several men living on her floor, says she is often awakened by loud knocking on her door at two or three o'clock in the morning. Another woman woke up one morning and found a stack of pornographic magazines outside her door.

Mary Wilson, an attractive woman of seventy-nine, describes how she was propositioned one day while she was walking toward the elevator after leaving her room: "This big, ugly man who is always drunk and dirty looking came out of his apartment as I went by and grabbed me by the arm. He said that if I went with him to his apartment he would stick his thing in my hole. He said he needed a girl and hadn't had one in a long time. I was scared to death but I told the son of a bitch to let go of me or I would scream. He did and I ran back to my room. Nowadays, whenever I need to go out, I look carefully both ways to make sure he isn't around.

In the prevention and control of threatening situations, staff members are sometimes called upon to help. When tenants complain to the manager about verbal shaming, threats of violence, racial slurs, or sexually insulting behavior she will intervene with threats of eviction if the evidence is convincing and if the protester doesn't have the reputation of being a chronic complainer. The security guard also intercedes in conflicts that occur in public areas (Table 1.1). On one occasion two men were exchanging personal insults in the lobby. Fearing violence, nearby observers quickly located the guard, who managed to separate the antagonists in time.

Concerns about the behavior of other residents are also the product of belief in the likelihood of cognitive decline with advancing age. Tenants share in general societal attitudes about increased mental deterioration in later life, and their fears are augmented by the fact of occupying the same living space with many in their late seventies and eighties. Behavior such as forgetfulness, getting off on the wrong floor, and talking to oneself is interpreted as evidence of mental decline. One hears frequent admonitions to keep away from the "crazy ones." Some think the place is turning into a kind of mental institution. Such beliefs make necessary interactions with nearby others seem unpredictable, on the supposition that even the behavior of likeable tenants might become obstreperous with the onset of physical and mental decline. Regardless of the truth, what is important is that tenants believe such changes can occur at any time. In a broader sense, then, the mere circumstance of age-segregated living can have an adverse effect on community interaction because, even though few exhibit irrational behavior, the prevailing attitude tends to be one of guarded watchfulness.

In other instances stereotypic beliefs about the behavior of minority-group members affect tenant interaction. Cohort effects are operative here. Born in an era when words such as "nigger," "kike," and "chink" were more acceptable in everyday usage, and having absorbed generalized notions about the characteristics of certain minorities, some residents reflect deeply ingrained prejudices that have resisted change. Conversations are liberally sprinkled with discriminatory terms, and minority-group members sometimes receive uncomplimentary nicknames.

Some of the white women are apprehensive about the increasing numbers of black men in the building. One woman thus described to me her reasons for moving out: "They're letting in so many of these old colored men that I'm ashamed to keep on living here. I went out in the hall not long ago to empty my garbage, and this Negro man who just moved in came out at the same time. He said, 'Hiya neighbor. How's everything going?' He had no right to speak to me like that, so I just walked by. This place has changed so much. When you go through the lobby it's filled with these old Negro men who do nothing but sit and look at you as you walk by."

In contrast, two studies concerned with the impact of ethnicity on the social organization of public housing for the aged reveal relatively harmonious interaction among divergent ethnic groups living in the same facility. Although Anglo, black, and Cuban residents of a public housing complex in North Miami maintain distinctive, ethnically defined subgroupings, relations between the groups are positive and do not appear to reflect the same degree of suspicion and prejudice prevalent in the outside community (Kandel and Heider 1979). Similarly, Wellin and Boyer (1979) found friendly interracial relations among the elderly tenants of a public housing apartment complex located in Milwaukee in which 40 percent of the resident population are black. Although the white tenants there evidence apprehension about the changing racial composition of the surrounding neighborhood, in which the black population is rapidly increasing, residential proximity and frequent contacts undermine racial barriers and promote mutual good will within the complex in contrast to racial fears on the outside. Such findings suggest that commonalities of age and residence may transcend patterns of prejudice and social separation in the task of building a viable, cohesive community.

Although residents frequently expressed prejudiced attitudes toward minority-group members of the St. Regis population and although distinct subgroupings based on race are clearly evident, relations between these groups are rarely disruptive. Yet the degree of interaction appears to be less than in the studies I have just cited. General community norms of noninvolvement are influential here. Black as well as white members are concerned about the privacy in their daily activities. Although many prefer to interact sociably with ethnically similar others contacts and exchanges of assistance are not limited by boundaries of ethnicity. Nor do the small numbers of black, Asiatic, and Hispanic residents pose much of a threat to the social dominance of the white segment. Many white tenants are also accustomed to sharing the same living space with minority-group members because of former residence in downtown hotels and apartments. In spite of frequent discriminatory comments, similar survival concerns often supersede racial intolerance, and the presence of minority groups is an accepted fact of daily existence.

Distancing Strategies

Beliefs about the dubious character of other tenants and the continuing presence of some who are considered dangerous cause a number of residents to use a variety of distancing procedures. Many feel that preventive actions by staff members are inadequate, so they often cope with troublemakers in their own way. Social ostracism is an effective technique. For example, after the previously described fight between two men in the elevator, there were several formal hearings and the Housing Authority finally decided to allow the offending tenant to remain, on probation. He had few family ties and his small income limited his ability to obtain decent accommodations elsewhere. A number of tenants were angered by the decision and interpreted it as further proof that management cared little about their welfare. As a result, few gave the offender any sign of recognition as he went about the building. Within several months he was rarely seen, for he increasingly altered his activities to avoid the embarassment of being ignored. The success of this strategy was evident in the comment of one resident that the "troublemaker" must have moved out because she hadn't seen him in such a long time.

Some tenants use alternate routes such as the backstairs and alley in going about their daily affairs; others avoid going through the lobby at times when it is known to be crowded. One woman who is particularly apprehensive about chance meetings with several male tenants that she dislikes describes the way she copes with her situation: "There are two men here whose mouths are so foul that if I get on the elevator and they are on it, I just turn around and go back to my room. Other times I get off on the third floor and go out the back way. That way I can also keep out of the lobby because I don't like the bad remarks people make about you down there. I guess I'm seen pretty rarely around here.

One woman asked me the other day if I had just moved in. Now isn't that something when I've lived here for four years!"

Others avoid unwanted associations by picking up their mail late at night. Some pointedly pursue social activities on the outside, and numbers who routinely pass through the lobby when entering and leaving the building scrupulously avoid conversational involvement. "You get together too much with people around here and it only makes for trouble," one man comments.

Male residents will often avoid involvement with women living in the building and satisfy their needs for feminine companionship on the outside. One man visits a woman friend in San Diego on a monthly basis; another has dinner twice a week with his fiancée, who lives several blocks away. A seventy-eight-year-old man explains why he resists the advances of several women tenants: "I got women living on either side of me, and one of them was always coming over bringing me things like a piece of cake or some cookies. One time she even brought over a picture of herself when she was younger—but I don't really think it was her because she's so homely now. But I didn't encourage her. I just don't want to get involved. And a lot of guys here feel the same way. They keep away from the women because it can get to be too much of a thing. We don't need all the complications. A lot of the guys who need some action just get it some place else—that's all."

In these instances, distancing strategies reduce the number of potential conflicts and the number of occasions on which verbal shaming and physical harm can occur. Social order is thus assured in a population unfamiliar with the techniques of cooperative living. Negative attitudes toward other tenants provide justification for social separateness and contribute to the preservation of private behavioral styles under circumstances where all must share the same living space.[6]

Friends and Lovers

Although many avoid personal involvement with other residents, there do exist between some tenants close relations that satisfy need for intimacy, provide companionship on recreational outings, and supply assistance in times of crisis. For example, Bernice Hanson and Ethel Miller became good friends when they lived in an old hotel close to the St. Regis. When their rent was increased, they decided to move to the St. Regis, where they have apartments on the same floor. Both are widowed, have few family ties, and enjoy relatively good health. Each year they spend several pleasant weeks touring such places as British Columbia, the East Coast, and New Orleans. Occasionally they double-date with two men living in the building. Recently Ethel became seriously ill and was taken to the hospital. Bernice visited her every day and provided housekeeping assistance briefly after Ethel was well enough to return home.

Roger Bacon is one of the oldest tenants in the building and admits to the age of ninety-one. He is friendly with four other male tenants, and the group spends many hours in the lobby exchanging comments about world events, sports, and residents who pass by. Several times a week they have dinner together in a favorite restaurant and return for a poker game that can last into the small hours. On one occasion Roger failed to answer his phone at a time when it was known he should be in his apartment. Within a few minutes a member of the group went to check on him and discovered Roger lying on the floor in severe pain from a heart attack. An ambulance was called and he was admitted to the hospital in time. Later he told me that if it hadn't been for the timely intervention of his friends, he probably would have died.

Some of the women maintain close relations with male tenants. In commenting on her friendship with a man living on the same floor, one resident described how she often took him portions of home-cooked beef stew and corned beef because of her concern about his dietary habits. She also buys food bargains for him during her weekly shopping expeditions, and he reciprocates by occasionally taking her out to dinner. When I asked if she envisioned a relationship that might become more serious, she quickly explained that she had already buried two husbands and had to nurse the last one for five years. She had had enough of "that kind of thing." But at least it was nice to "do for a man" occasionally and enjoy his company.

In other situations a few men and women have remained un-concerned about exposure to gossip and have established deeply affectionate, quasi-spousal affiliations. Beatrice and Isaac, both in their eighties, have been close companions for ten years. Both are widowed but have rejected the idea of marriage because of wanting to preserve some degree of individual privacy. During periods of hospitalization they visit each other regularly—an act often involving bus rides of an hour and a half each way. When Beatrice returned from the hospital after a second operation for cancer, Isaac cooked and cleaned for her in spite of his chronic ar-thritis, and she was able to avoid a period of recuperation in a convalescent home. Soon afterward, Beatrice related to me how she stayed up one night putting hot compresses on Isaac's legs when he was experiencing a bad attack of arthritic pain. Al-though both have grown children in the area, it is to one another that they turn in time of need.

Involvement in these close relationships can entail heavy affec-tive costs when death occurs. I encountered an example of this one day when I came upon Harriet Simons, an eighty-one-year-old woman, sitting on a couch outside the manager's office, cry-ing and rocking back and forth. When I asked if there was any-thing I could do, she related how her dear friend Mr. Hopkins had died in the hospital that morning.

> I did my best to take care of him. We've shared a lot in the last couple of years. We used to go away on trips, and he'd take me out to dinner at least once a week. When he got so sick, I kept his apartment clean and did all his errands. But he didn't get any better, and when he couldn't eat anymore I persuaded him to go to the hospital. I think he knew he wasn't going to make it back. When the ambulance came he just held my hand tightly and told me how much I meant to him. But it is God's will that he was taken. The Lord takes us in his own time and according to his own plan. I should be happy about the time we were able to have together.

That some residents form deeply caring relationships with oth-ers entailing both risks of loss in the event of death and mutual benefits in the satisfaction of intimacy needs, illustrates the heterogeneity of sociable preferences that indeed influences the quality of community life at the St. Regis. But as the discussion in this chapter has shown, limited interpersonal involvement is the preferred mode of interaction. The lack of close ties is not necessarily indicative of social pathology; it can also be interpreted as representing habitual modes of involvement that have changed little over the years. It is the relative absence of intimate bonds and the behavioral patterns reinforcing social distance between members that enable this collectivity to function effectively.

Thus a large group of individualistically oriented men and women are able to live together in relative harmony and benefit from the advantages of increased access to assistance and from the greater protectiveness that collective living in these circumstances provides. The social contract between tenants is best described in terms of survival concerns, and it is on this basis that the community functions as a cohesive unit.

Chapter 3

The Gender Gap

In the St. Regis, men outnumber women three to one. These proportions are the reverse of many retirement communities, where female dominance is the norm, but they are similar to other SRO populations in skid-row and working-class hotels in downtown areas (Ehrlich 1976; Erickson and Eckert 1977; Stephens 1976). What are the implications of this skewed distribution in relation to the comparative life histories and adaptive capacities of men and women residents? Do the small numbers of women imply that men are more capable of adapting to and coping with the urban milieu, where documented survival skills emphasizing self-reliance, utilitarian values, and nonintimacy would appear to be more valuable than traditional female roles stressing dependence and expressive behavior? In particular, do these women experience a sense of discontinuity with former domestic roles and a psychosocial alienation in a male-dominated environment?

A scarcity of information inhibits valid comparisons between the survival skills of aged men and women living in the inner city. Investigations of the SRO elderly frequently base their findings on populations that are dominated by men (Erickson and Eckert 1977; Stephens 1976), and the few studies that describe urban elderly women reveal contrasting perspectives. For example, in Shapiro's (1971) study of nine SRO hotels in New York, a frequent constellation consisted of quasi-families headed by a black elderly woman. Such women partially adhered to traditional women's roles by providing nurturance, discipline, and material aid to small groups of dependent, often alcoholic men. In another study of an SRO setting in Detroit, Stephens

(1974) postulated that the aged women who lived there were ill equipped to adapt successfully to the exploitive impersonal milieu of the SRO. These women experienced a sense of severe discontinuity with earlier conventional roles emphasizing marriage and children. Homemaking and nurturing behavior found little opportunity for expression in their male-dominated world. Locked into a no-exit situation because of poverty, scarce family ties, and ill health, female residents were more vulnerable to the consequences of social isolation and often withdrew into a fantasized past in which they viewed themselves as still being incorporated into loving family groups. In their present circumstances, they could find little opportunity for self-validation based on a former status.

The findings, however, in a more recent study (Lally et al. 1979) of the life histories of sixteen older women living singly in hotels in the Seattle area question former views of entrapment and helplessness. In contrast to Stephens' (1974) investigation, residence in the central city for these women appeared to be a consequence of solitary, independent lives in which values of self-sufficiency, privacy, and autonomy played pivotal roles. Most had been salaried employees during their adults years, and half had worked in male-dominated occupations. Their educational levels were significantly higher than national averages for their age peers, and two had been teachers. At least one-third had lived in downtown hotels for many years, and the majority viewed their present living arrangements as a matter of personal choice. Stated advantages of downtown living emphasized the convenience of department stores, lower rents, and opportunities for privacy and independence. Although most had been married at one time, family contacts were constrained and conflictual.

Another informative perspective is offered by Gubrium (1975), who intensively studied twenty-two never-married, elderly men and women residing in a variety of housing arrangements in Detroit. In old age, this group did not experience the sense of deprivation resulting from social and personal losses that is frequently associated with growing older. Intensive interviews revealed that they were experiencing a sense of continuity, rather than discontinuity, with earlier lifestyles that were characterized by minimal involvement in friendship and familial networks. Years of independent living and minimal social ties probably resulted in less dependence on significant others for self-validation compared with age peers in more traditional relationships. Consequently, such people may be less vulnerable to the depressive consequences of personal and social losses accompanying the aging process. Although the responses were not differentiated according to sex, such findings lend support to the contention that coping strategies in later life can be the product of situational contingencies extending over the life-span and are not necessarily determined by the socializing influences of sex-role prescriptions.

Given similar life experiences including years of singlehood and independent living, it is reasonable to assume that both women and men may evidence comparable skills in coping with the challenges of daily life in the inner city. I am not ignoring or denying the presence in these surroundings of women who, by virtue of lifelong involvement in domestic roles, lack the necessary coping capacities for meaningful survival and spend their days in fear and isolation. But in the St. Regis I came across members of both sexes who were equally at home in the inner city, exhibiting survival capabilities tempered by years of autonomous living in urban surroundings.

The life experiences of men and women at the St. Regis exhibit many similarities, although idiosyncratic differences certainly exist. As previous discussion has shown, the majority of both sexes are either widowed, separated, or divorced and have been living alone for a number of years. Eschewing traditional feminine roles emphasizing sociability skills, many of the women are similar to the men in their lifelong avoidance of commitment to personal relationships and in the values they place on privacy and autonomy. Parallel patterns are also present in their work histories. In addition to meeting familial obligations, many women tenants have also worked in semiskilled and marginal occupations through choice or necessity and have been self-supporting for most of their adult years. Many also have chosen to remain downtown to preserve continuity with former urban lifestyles and to benefit from the advantages of being centrally located.

Similarities also exist in the diversity of life histories and interactional patterns of both sexes. In contradistinction to the SRO values of self-reliance and limited social relationships that provide the dominant ideological underpinnings for the conduct of daily affairs in this setting, some men and women exhibit nurturing behavior, involvement in community affairs, and concern for the maintenance of family ties.

The following representative case histories demonstrate the comparability of lifestyles and values among men and women residents in addition to the heterogeneity that is also an integral part of the St. Regis scene. In spite of individual differences, the personal histories of Malcolm MacDonald, Rosemary Barker, and Marian Cummings are typified by minimal involvement in family relationships, years of independent living, and avoidance of intimate ties. In old age, they consistently seek to maintain a sense of congruence with earlier living modes exemplifying autonomy and self-reliance. Contrasting perspectives appear in the shorter vignettes describing the circumstances of several men and women who are more closely involved with friends and family and who maintain an active interest in community events. These tenants also prefer, however, to live independently in the downtown area and take pride in their remaining capacities for self-sufficiency.

Malcolm MacDonald

Malcolm was born in Scotland in 1893. He came from a working-class background and had little formal schooling. During World War I, he enlisted in the British navy, and when the hostilities ended, he became a merchant seaman. In this capacity he traveled to many parts of the world and enjoyed a reputation for being a heavy drinker and an expert with the ladies. During these years he married and had four children, three sons and a daughter. Two of his sons lost their lives in World War II; one son and the daughter are still living in England. In his late thirties, he emigrated to the United States, leaving his family behind. For a number of years he worked as a tile setter in different construction jobs for the navy and lived in several cities along the West Coast.

Upon retirement at the age of 65, he settled on several acres adjacent to an Indian reservation in the Pacific Northwest, where he led a quiet life growing vegetables and raising several cows. Life was good in those days. "I used to get these squaws coming around and I could get anything I wanted anytime I wanted it." Tiring of the wet winters, he decided to move to Los Angeles in the mid-1960s to take advantage of the warmer climate. For years he lived in a hotel in the inner city and finally moved to the St. Regis when the building he was living in was demolished to make room for a shopping center. He has no personal assets except for social security and SSI benefits.

In both dress and physical appearance Malcolm is a distinctive figure in any group. He is a large, heavy-set man with an expansive stomach that protrudes prominently over a belt that seems too small. Sparse white hair frames an angular face that is pale and heavily lined. Blue eyes peer out from under thick eyebrows that dominate his face. His cheeks are sunken, and he rarely smiles because of his dislike of wearing his ill-fitting dentures. Invariably, Malcolm appears around the building in the same costume: a bright red woolen stocking cap perched on his head, shiny black pants worn over high black boots badly in need of repair, and a plaid shirt. He expresses considerable concern for his health and says he suffers from high blood pressure, heart problems, and chronic diabetes. His eyesight is severely limited and a white cane is constantly by his side. His recreation is attending the races, walking the downtown streets, and taking a bus to the Central Market several times a week, where he spends enjoyable hours selecting meats and vegetables at bargain prices. He takes great pride in his culinary expertise, and much of his conversation contains descriptions of favorite recipes.

Relationships with friends and relatives are sparse, conflictual, and exploitive. Any mention of his family in England elicits angry comments on not wanting to be involved. "They don't care anything about me," he exclaims. "All they are interested in is my pension check." He claims that his children are a disappointment to him, and his other relatives are all "bastards." Never does he mention his reasons for leaving his wife and children in earlier years. Occasionally, he visits with one or two men who live in the neighborhood, but he does not refer to them as friends. At the St. Regis he is regarded as a character with a quick temper and a penchant for quarrelsome behavior. His general aloofness and often-stated dislike for other tenants has not endeared him to the rest of the population. Malcolm seems to thrive on his sense of difference and continually reminds others of his British origins. He states that he is now unable to have relationships with women but takes pride in the number of affairs he has had in the past. Women to him are, nonetheless, a source of trouble and "always want to get something out of you."

I was first introduced to Malcolm by the Housing Authority receptionist when I went to her office to obtain a list of new tenants to visit. As soon as I mentioned my Canadian background, he began to talk about his contempt for the British aristocracy and his disdain for the present royal family. He then asked if I had any children and whether or not my husband had been in the service. When I replied in the affirmative to both queries, he retorted that my children would be mean when they were teenagers. In his opinion, people in the armed forces "get all these shots that ruin your backbone and contaminate the body liquids." "Now," he continued, "these things get passed along in the sperm through intercourse and make problems for your kids when they grow up." When I expressed some surprise, he added that this is what is wrong with so many teenagers today. "Stop the shots and a lot of these problems with these young kids will eventually go away." I ventured that this was indeed an interesting explanation and one I hadn't heard before. He then picked up the vacuum cleaner he needed to borrow from the office and left. The receptionist was surprised I had gotten along so well with him because of his unfriendly reputation.

Several weeks later, I met Malcolm in the lobby on his way out. He was going to the Central Market and, in response to my expression of interest, invited me to go the next week. He insisted, however, that we meet in a restaurant down the street. He didn't want all those "duds and bastards" in the lobby to know about our plans. On the appointed day we drove in my car to the market—a fascinating and colorful place—dozens of food stalls in a large, enclosed area displaying a great variety of fruits, vegetables, and canned goods. Household items and clothing are also for sale at bargain prices. As we entered, I was struck by the number of elderly men and women walking around carrying shopping bags in the midst of a largely younger Hispanic crowd.

Gripping me tightly by the arm, Malcolm propelled me through the crowd and instructed me to hold on to my purse. We visited his favorite food stands, where he purchased several pounds of chicken wings, two cabbages, and some halibut. I noticed the prices were considerably below those I would pay in my own neighborhood supermarket. Malcolm was obviously enjoying himself, for this was his turf and he was well known. Several vendors referred to him by his first name, and in the spirited bargaining that followed, he was able to get the price of the cabbages reduced by twenty cents. I purchased some blue cheese that proved delicious. It was a happy afternoon and Malcolm was an entertaining and knowledgeable guide. As we drove back to the St. Regis, he had me let him out a block away, concerned again about gossip, should we be seen together.

A few weeks after this excursion I visited Malcolm for the first time in his apartment. It was immaculate. The stove and small kitchen counter were wiped clean; dishes were neatly arranged in the cupboard. Two glass vases filled with plastic flowers that had seen better days and several paper rosebuds attached to the mirror were the only personal touches I could see. As we talked, he told me details of his earlier life, including an affair with a woman about fifteen years ago. He managed to avoid marriage but in the process was able to get some money from her. He chuckled as he described how he "had gotten the better of her."

Malcolm then turned to his problems with his next door neighbor. This man was driving him crazy. (I noticed that he never referred to this person by name.) His neighbor constantly woke him up at night by playing the TV and banging around in his room. Malcolm didn't like him because this man considered himself better than other people living in the building. "Who does he think he is, looking down his nose at everybody?" Giving further testimony attesting to the despicable character of this man, he described how his neighbor had taken some home-baked biscuits to a "nice little woman" who lived on the same floor. But in return for this gesture, the neighbor requested a "little action." The woman, Malcolm said, was horrified and refused. He felt nothing but contempt for this man's attempt to take advantage of "the poor old lady" in that way.

The following week I again visited Malcolm in his room. When I arrived, he was beginning to prepare his noon meal of a succulent piece of round steak, which he was cooking slowly under the broiler. A sliced onion sat on top of the meat, along with several tablespoons of bacon fat. The aroma was delicious. He mentioned that he had not been feeling well. He was short of breath and felt tired much of the time, but these problems were not going to stand in the way of his plan to attend the races on the next day. He was at the moment deeply involved in picking out potential winners. Not wanting to interrupt this important activity, I left shortly.

As I continued to see Malcolm intermittently over the next few months, he became increasingly agitated toward his neighbor. He was concerned that the "old man" was trying to get into his room to kill him. Several mornings he awoke to find his door unlocked. But he had evolved a plan to protect himself. He would go to the hardware store and buy two eye bolts—one to be attached to the door and the other to be fastened to the wall. Once he tied a rope across, there would be no way anyone could enter without his knowledge.

Concerned about the extent of his anger, I asked if he could request to have his room changed. He shrugged in a futile manner, saying he had already submitted a request to the Housing Authority that had been denied. All the "niggers" who were coming into the St. Regis these days were getting rooms, but he was unable to do so. Malcolm was bitterly prejudiced against blacks and regarded them as dirty and uneducated. He rudely brushed aside any comments I made in disagreement.

About a month later he invited me to have lunch in his apartment. When I arrived I noticed that for once he was wearing his dentures. My acceptance of his invitation must have been an important event. The first part of the visit was devoted to the ceremony of deboning the chicken. Malcolm showed much expertise, and I watched as he deftly severed the wings and legs from the carcass. I had the feeling he was in surgery and I was the assistant handing him different instruments. He removed the breast meat by guiding his thumb along the breastbone and pushing downward. Once this was done, he brought out an oven-proof platter that already had some grease in the bottom. Laying the chicken breasts on top, he covered the pieces with onions and bacon grease and placed the dish under the broiler for twenty minutes. He removed the platter, covered the other side of the breasts with cloves and chopped garlic, and returned the chicken to the oven for another twenty minutes. The meal was excellent. We ate this along with coffee made from scratch by placing grounds in boiling water.

As we talked, the topic of conversation reverted to his earlier days, and he recounted a story that occurred when he was living on his small farm in Washington State. He considered himself an expert on many matters, and his knowledge included innovative theories about breeding cows. He bought a skinny cow appropriately called "Miss Bones" from one of his neighbors. The original owner had tried to breed her many times without success. Malcolm proceeded to fatten her up and was finally able to breed her successfully to a good bull. "You can't breed a cow when she comes in from the field in the late afternoon all hot and upset. You have to wait until the cow is cold. This happens around eleven or twelve at night. Then the cow is settled down and content. But when she's all hot and upset, all the sperm get burnt up and expelled." Eleven months later the cow gave birth to a healthy calf. Malcolm advocated that women who had difficulty in getting pregnant follow similar instructions.

In the two or three months that followed, Malcolm experienced increased health problems. On two occasions he was hospitalized briefly to undergo extensive tests related to circulatory and digestive disorders. One day I visited him in the hospital to take him some support bandages he customarily used for his knees so as to feel more secure in walking around. When I arrived he was very appreciative and said, in his still distinguishable Scottish brogue, "God bless you, girl." After he wrapped his legs, we took a walk down the hospital corridor, Malcolm leaning heavily on my shoulder for support and stopping frequently to rest. He spoke of the importance of getting enough exercise; to him, this was an important way of keeping up his strength. The receptionist had been to see him several times, he said, bringing some personal items from his room. In addition, his arch enemy who lived next door had been down to visit him the day before. Malcolm described the visit tersely saying that all the "old bastard" did was to come into his room, mutter a few unintelligible comments, and leave. Before I left, he remarked that he was now tired of living and wished he could die and "get it all over with." But then, with a wink and a smile, he added that maybe he wasn't quite finished yet.

The following week Malcolm was back at the St. Regis. When I went to visit him in his room, he was lying on top of his bed fully clothed, wearing his ever-present knitted cap. He looked pale and had lost some weight. Because of continuing indigestion, he was only able to tolerate easily digestible foods. He mentioned that the receptionist was looking in on him each day and "some other guy" was buying his groceries. In spite of his professed antagonism toward others in the building, Malcolm's support system seemed to be intact and operating effectively.

Several weeks later, Malcolm had recovered to the point of being able to resume some of his customary daily activities. He was now able to catch the bus to make trips to Central Market and was even contemplating an excursion to the racetrack. But in spite of these improvements, he continued to complain about his poor health. One day when I met him in the lobby, he said he didn't feel his heart could go on much longer . . . he was getting close to the end. But at least now he could take care of himself and didn't have to depend on anyone else.

It was also at this point that Malcolm's relationship with me became problematic. He wanted me to ask the Housing Authority to repair some of his furniture and give him new drapes.

When I explained that our counseling service was not able to intervene in landlord–tenant affairs, he responded angrily that he could see I was too busy to be bothered with his needs. After this, he refused to let me in his apartment on several occasions, reiterating that I probably had more important things to do. During the following year, my efforts to mend the break in our relationship were futile, and Malcolm refused to give me any sign of recognition during chance encounters.

I was initially hurt by this rejection because I had become fond of this irrascible Scotsman. Only later did I come to understand that maintaining a close relationship with anyone was incompatible with his adversarial style of relating to significant others. When I finally left the St. Regis, Malcolm was continuing to experience some cardiac and digestive problems. He moved more slowly, but with the aid of his cane he was still able to attend the races occasionally and venture down to the Central Market at least once a week.

Rosemary Barker

I came in contact with Rosemary after I had been in the setting for six months. We became good friends, and she shared with me many details of her personal life and activities during quiet talks in her nicely furnished apartment. She has played out her life script in opposition to traditional feminine roles, and she considers herself a "city woman." Assertiveness, a single lifestyle, and a high degree of self-reliance are the salient themes of her personal history.

Rosemary was Caucasian, born in Boston in 1901. Her childhood years were filled with tragedy and instability. When she was five, her mother and father were killed in an accident, leaving Rosemary and two younger sisters to be raised by several aunts and uncles. One sister died of an undiagnosed illness shortly afterward, and the other ran away at the age of sixteen. To the end, Rosemary never so much as heard whether her sister was dead or alive. Rosemary attended a succession of boarding schools, spending school vacations with alternate relatives. At sixteen she married an older man; within five years he died, leaving her with a daughter and no means of support. Several years later she married again, but her second husband was physically abusive and she quickly divorced him. Faced with a young child to raise, she obtained a job in the clothing industry and worked her way up to the point of managing a chain of several small retail stores. Eventually her daughter married and moved to the West Coast.

Around 1960 Rosemary left her position to come to Los Angeles to be close to her daughter. She obtained a clerical job in a department store in downtown Los Angeles and moved into a small housekeeping room near work. In 1965 she suffered a stroke and sustained some paralysis on her left side. Although she recovered rapidly, she decided she was unable to return to work. Feeling that she would be able to live on a small pension and her social security income, she remained in the apartment building where she had been staying until a rental increase necessitated a move into the St. Regis.

In appearance, Rosemary was of average height and had a thin, wiry build. Abundant gray hair cut in a short style outlined a sharp-featured face with bright, blue eyes. She wore minimal makeup and dressed in a neat, conservative fashion. Filled with a type of nervous energy that is expressed in rapid, darting movements and hurried speech, she was constantly active, her days filled with an assortment of activities: numerous errands to department stores, altering and mending clothing for tenants in return for a small fee, and visiting one or two friends.

The themes of tragedy and loss continued to pervade her personal relationships. Several years after she moved to Los Angeles, her daughter committed suicide. She never spoke of the circumstances, but whenever the subject came up, her eyes filled with tears and she lapsed into poignant silence. Her relationship with her one grandson, who was in his twenties, was tenuous. He visited occasionally, but she maintained he was only interested in borrowing money and showed little concern for her well-being. Except for exchanges of notes at Christmas, she had little contact with relatives on the East Coast.

One day shortly after we met, she invited me to her apartment for a cup of tea. Her room was attractively furnished and filled with handmade items that attested to her sewing skills. Crocheted potholders hung above the stove; embroidered pillows added pleasing touches of color to the couch; and a handmade rug hung from the wall. She proudly showed me her latest project, converting cigar boxes into jewelry cases by covering them with felt, glitter, and sequins. Occasionally she sold such items to other residents. Although she didn't make much money, receiving something in return for her investment of time and money was important to her. On an ironing board set up on one side of the room was a dress she was altering for a neighbor down the hall. "I only get two dollars for doing this," she said, "but I don't feel I should do it for free."

As we talked, Rosemary spoke of the many advantages of downtown living. Everything was close by, and when she wanted to visit one close friend, she was able to catch a bus right outside the door. But she expressed concern about the number of muggings and robberies in the inner city. "The black kids come down here and prey off we old people." Nonetheless, Rosemary thought she knew how to take care of herself out on the streets. "I've lived around here for a long time and I know the ropes. When I see a black or Mexican kid coming my way, I keep my elbow sticking out so I can jab them if they try to get too close. I also keep a whistle around my neck to blow in case someone tries to rob me." She went on to describe another measure for protecting herself against ciminal victimization: at night she never opens her door to anyone, and if someone is coming over, she requests that he or she call beforehand.

About a month later I went to her apartment to look at some scraps of material she wanted to donate to the crafts group sponsored by our counseling service. On this occasion we talked about her views concerning other tenants. Touching on a familiar theme that reflected opinions held by many in the building, she spoke disparagingly about the low character of some who lived on her floor and those who wasted their days sitting in the lobby. With some relish, she went on to recount an incident that illustrated her capacity for looking after herself. About six years earlier, when she was living in another apartment building, she had accepted a dinner invitation from a man she barely knew. "When he took me back to my apartment, he said he wanted to come in to see the kind of place I lived in. I shouldn't have let him. He threw me on the bed and tried to get on top of me. Then I remembered what my husband said years ago if anyone tried to do something to me. [She got up to demonstrate her story.] I got him right in his private parts [raising her knee]. Oh . . . he got up, doubled over and called me every name in the book. But then he got out, so I was O.K." Laughing, she added that even though she was old, she was still strong enough to handle herself.

There was a knock at the door, and a tall, stout man entered, carrying a dish of sauerkraut and sausages. Rosemary introduced him as "Bill," her next door neighbor, and added that they often exchanged recipes and special dishes. Her neighbor laughed and said that this time he had come up with something that was "really good." Rosemary tasted the sauerkraut (a little gingerly I thought) and thanked him warmly. Her friend was unable to stay because of a prior commitment and left in a few minutes. After he was gone, Rosemary confided that she couldn't eat much of the food he brought because it was too heavily spiced. But she would never tell him that because it would hurt his feelings. "Now that is a very nice man," she added. "He's a perfect gentleman and has the nicest manners. But he also has a drinking problem. He drinks several six-packs and some of that hard stuff all in one day. That's enough to kill anybody." Recently he had been sick and Rosemary had bought his groceries and picked up his mail. She refused, however, to buy him any liquor. "He looks so much better now. But I know he isn't going to stay off the stuff." I complimented her on these acts of helpfulness. She responded that he was worth helping because, even drunk, he was still pleasant and a good talker.

Three months later, Bill moved to a public housing project on the other side of the city to be close to a married son. He died shortly afterward from an unexpected heart attack, and Rosemary expressed grief over his death. "He was a nice old codger, but I shouldn't have let myself get to like him so much because when they're old like that, they just up and die on you."

Although still physically active, Rosemary began to experience occasional chest pains and severe vertigo, but these problems didn't prevent her from following a busy round of activities and she refused to remain closeted in her room. I began to hear stories that she was drinking heavily, although she never mentioned it in our conversations. One day she appeared in my office with substantial bruises on her face and arms. She had fallen in her apartment and lost consciousness for several hours. For three days she remained in the hospital before returning home under orders to follow a strict regimen of rest and quiet. But she became impatient with her program of care and medication and felt the pills she was taking did little good.

She continued to visit her favorite department stores and see a friend occasionally. As the months went by, though, declining energy necessitated some curtailment of her daily pursuits, forcing her to spend more time in her apartment. One day as I was visiting her shortly before I left the setting, she told me she wanted to die in her own room and had few regrets about her past life. "I've always been able to look after myself and now it's God's turn," she added. Several months later I received word that Rosemary had died quietly in her sleep in her room. Her grandson appeared to claim her personal effects and sign necessary papers.

Marian Cummings

Marian is a seventy-six-year-old outgoing Caucasian woman who moved into the St. Regis in 1977. Over the years, her lifestyle has also reflected nonadherence to conventional female roles, preferences for independent urban living, and a lack of commitment to lasting relationships. She appears much younger than her years and dresses modishly. Her hair is dyed a soft shade of red and worn in a short style that curls attractively around her face. She is slim and takes pride in the youthful curves of her figure. Diet and exercise are important aspects of her daily schedule, and she will only eat organic health foods and well-trimmed meat. She perceives herself as being in good health, although she occasionally admits to some arthritis and minor heart ailments.

During our acquaintance she was circumspect about the details of her early life and rarely spoke of her family relationships and marital involvements, although she did say she had a brother and sister still living somewhere in the East. Her contacts with these siblings are minimal and limited to exchanges of Christmas cards. She married and divorced at an early age and later married another man, who constantly traveled to major cities. During this marriage, she lived in a succession of apartment buildings and hotels, rarely staying longer that a year or two in each place, a rootless existence she liked. She said living out of suitcases prevented accumulation of unnecessary possessions. This second husband died after ten years, leaving Marian with a small annuity that has lasted up to the present.

In the intervening years, Marian gradually moved toward the West Coast, living in several large cities and occasionally working as a receptionist or salesclerk. She becomes restless if she remains in one area too long and prefers the excitement of meeting new people and tasting the flavor of different cities across the country. Having arrived in Los Angeles several years ago, she feels she will remain, for the warm sun and the access to the beach.

In spite of her congenial nature Marian has few friends, probably because of the unsettled nature of her existence. Several men have expressed interest in marriage, but Marian resists committing herself to any kind of permanent arrangement. She doesn't want to spend her later years looking after "some old geezer" who would only get sick and die. She assiduously avoids having anything to do with the male tenants and refers to them disparagingly as "skid-row types." Yet she confidentially states that she still has sexual needs that are met by several "nice men" who live on the outside.

I first met Marian at the monthly coffee party several weeks after she moved in. As we talked, she gave her initial impressions of the other tenants: "None of them seem to do anything . . . they just sit around and atrophy. Now I like to be always going out and doing something. That's the key to keeping in good health and good spirits." She also told me she had special powers and considered herself a spiritual healer, but she didn't want this information to get around because people might consider her to be "funny."

·Several weeks later Marian extended an invitation to eat lunch in her apartment. Her room was in a comfortable state of clutter, clothes flung carelessly over the furniture. I could see few items of a personal nature and an open suitcase half-filled with clothes in one corner. We sat down to lunch of a cup of beef broth purchased from a health food store and a dessert of boiled dried apricots. As we talked, Marian continually got out of her chair to show me different items of interest. As an avid collector of antique jewelry and sea shells, one of her favorite pastimes is to attending white elephant sales at churches, where she can find old jewelry at bargain prices. To illustrate her success, she carefully brought over a box containing a pair of delicate filigreed silver earrings that she claimed were authentic antiques. She also loves to travel by bus to beach areas and pick up assorted shells. Items like these are small and can easily be carried when she moves.

After lunch, I happened to mention that I was tired and feeling somewhat depressed. Immediately, Marian asked if I wanted her to use her healing powers to make me feel better. Rather hesitantly I agreed. Carefully she washed her hands, instructed me to sit in an armchair, and requested that I close my eyes. She then applied her fingers gently to my head, face, and throat and began a prayer in which she invoked the powers of God and Allah to surround me with "the great white light" that would penetrate me and heal all the sickness in my body. She asked these deities to allow the healing power to go through her fingers into my body. (Indeed, I was beginning to feel a warm sensation spreading through my body, and I found myself wondering about the powers of suggestion.) The session was terminated by an appeal to Allah for his blessings and protection. I told her that I was now feeling much better and offered my thanks. Pleased by my response, she said she had been wondering if she had lost this power she was born with. Several nights before, she had given a healing session to another woman tenant who did not seem to benefit; now, she was reassured.

During the next few months Marian became friendly with Mary Phillips, a quiet woman who was moving back to Kentucky to be closer to a sister. She wanted Mary to sell some of her belongings and couldn't understand why she refused to part with these possessions. "I believe you should get rid of anything you don't need when you move and get cash for them," she insisted. She also planned to give Mary a going-away party in the lobby. A notice about the event was placed on the bulletin board in the lobby, and Marian ordered a large cake. Going around the building trying to get signatures on a card, she experienced difficulty in getting people to sign their names. Disgustedly, she told me she was only able to get about a dozen signatures. "Can you imagine that?" A lot of the guys I asked either refused or wouldn't talk to me. They make me so mad!" On the day of the affair, most of the people sitting in the lobby accepted a piece of cake, but only a few seemed to know what the occasion was.

Intermittently, Marian attended some of the arts and crafts sessions, but she finds it difficult to commit herself to a regularly scheduled event. On one particular day the topic of conversation centered around the questionable character of some of the male tenants. "Some of these old boys around here are really out to get you," Marian commented, "but I can handle most of them." To illustrate her point she recounted the following story. "You know old so and and so . . . the one who dances around all the time? I can't stand him. He tried to grab me the other day and whirl me around when I was going through the lobby. I told him to keep his paws to himself." As far as she was concerned, he didn't have the "pause that refreshes." The other women laughed appreciatively and Marian continued: "Now, I know that some are nice and just want to be friends. But most are out to get you," she repeated. She described another invitation from one of her neighbors, to have a cup of coffee in his apartment. She refused, telling him she knew there was just one thing he wanted. Now she avoided even talking to any of the men in the lobby because of the gossip that could result. "Talk to anyone around here and all those people who sit around have you in bed together. I don't stop anymore or talk to anybody."

A few weeks later she dropped by my office for a few minutes of conversation. Marian said she wasn't "all there today." She had been out in astro-space since eight o'clock that morning and hadn't yet come all the way back. This made her mind foggy and it was difficult for her to think clearly. "Oh yes, I take many journeys into outer space, leaving my body behind and letting my mind float free and clear. Sometimes I'm so happy out there I just don't want to come back." She then went on to discuss whether or not she was going to stay in her apartment. She liked living downtown because she had lived in cities most of her life and felt able to take care of herself, but living around all these "old fogies" was depressing. The other day in the lobby some man had accused her of being one of the worst gossips in the building. She had become incensed but quickly rationalized that he was probably senile.

In several months, when I returned from a vacation, I learned from another counselor that Marian had moved out after living in the building for ten months. A few days later I ran into her in the lobby as she was returning to pick up a few things. When I expressed surprise that she had moved so quickly, she explained that she had unexpectedly received a little money and was able to afford a better apartment. She was now in a nice building close to the downtown area and had access to a swimming pool. "This place was beginning to bore me," she added, "and I needed something different. They're all dead around here." Later contacts with Marian in her new surroundings revealed that she was again becoming discontented. Change and variability are the necessary ingredients in her restless way of life.

The Reality of Diversity

Although the foregoing case histories exemplify lifestyles and world views typical of many residents, variation in backgrounds and adaptive patterns are also in evidence. Some men and women have numerous friends, warm family ties, and an active interest in community events. Several women are disheveled and appear to be mentally confused. As long as their requests for assistance are not excessive and their behavior is not disruptive, these women occupy an exempt status in which confused actions are excused by such explanations as "The poor lady isn't all there and doesn't know what she's doing half the time." In some instances, a few male tenants offer protection and assistance.

An example of this occurred in a relationship that developed between Charles Mason, a recognized leader in the community, and Mary Chow, a tiny, unprepossessing woman in her early seventies who was born in China and emigrated to this country as a young girl. Although claiming to be a college graduate, she is obviously financially destitute in old age and has lived in a nearby hotel for several years before coming to the St. Regis. Her clothing is in a continual state of disarray. She most often appears in a dark housedress, a ragged sweater, and stockings rolled below the knee. Constantly by her side is a worn leather suitcase that contains the remnants of her past identity. To anyone stopping to talk, she will quickly show a yellowed diploma from the University of Chicago, a Time-Life book with pictures of ancient Chinese paintings, a photo taken when she was a young girl, and a small Chinese tapestry of ancient origins. Her conversation is interspersed with vague references to God, and topics are frequently unrelated. Names, places, and dates are difficult for her to remember and she confuses past and present events.

When she first arrived, Mr. Mason became her self-appointed sponsor, introducing her to other tenants as the "nice little lady from China who has a college degree." Because of her limited English and confused manner of speaking, he often intervened and attempted to explain to others what she meant to say. When she was having difficulty understanding the rental agreement, he provided assistance by accompanying her to the manager's office. On another occasion when I was going through the lobby, he purposely called me over and suggested that we should invite Miss Chow to join the Arts and Crafts Club. Mary was profuse in her expressions of gratitude for his assistance and insisted at one point that he accept several watercolors of flowers that she had painted. Charles persisted in his attempts to defend her reputation and responded protectively when other tenants made critical comments about her "queer ways."

Close family ties are also maintained by some men, although distancing elements are often present. Gregory Roberts, a handsome black man who was a jazz musician in the south for many years, has frequent contacts with two married children living in Portland, Oregon. Although he was divorced many years ago and has been living alone for fifteen years, he visits his son and daughter at least twice a year and speaks of his grandchildren with pride. But he has resisted invitations to live with his daughter because of a professed wish to remain on his own. "This place I have here is my home," he once said, "and I'm always glad to get back."

For the past ten years, Gregory also maintained a quasi-spousal relationship with an elderly Caucasian woman who was in poor health. She lived in a more expensive apartment building in the downtown area and enjoyed a comfortable income. In addition to sexual companionship, he provided maintenance services such as grocery shopping and cleaned her living quarters once a week. When she died recently and made no provision for him in her will, he reacted with a mixture of sorrow and anger. He grieved over her loss because of strong feelings of attachment but also expressed bitter disappointment that she showed so little concern for his welfare: "After all I did for her, you'd think she'd leave me something."

In spite of publicly supported norms of noninvolvement in community affairs and criticism of those who occupy formal leadership roles, some men and women persist in their efforts to promote group activities. Although refusing to accept an official position, Charles Mason remains concerned about the lack of support for the Senior Citizens' Club and expends considerable effort to promote attendance at meetings and other social occasions such as the community dinners at Thanksgiving and Christmas. Similarly, I have cited Elaine Michael's continuing involvement in the biweekly bingo games, the Senior Citizens' Club, and planning tours to Las Vegas. In her past life she was a member of numerous organizations in which she held official positions. Becoming involved in similar activities at the St. Regis validates her past identity and reinforces her self-esteem. In spite of some criticism she receives for her efforts, she probably benefits from a greater degree of toleration because of her general popularity and social skills.

In contrast to many other tenants, Mrs. Michaels, at the age of seventy-eight, is also closely enmeshed in a viable network of family and friends. Although married at an early age and the mother of four children, Elaine worked for most of her married years in a clerical capacity. She was widowed at the age of fifty-two and has remained single although several men have proposed marriage. She didn't feel anyone could replace her deceased husband. For several years she lived with a married daughter, but a desire for greater independence prompted a move downtown for the convenience of cheaper rents and the easy accessibility to transportation and retail stores. She frequently visits one son in New Mexico and spends weekends with a married daughter on the outskirts of Los Angeles.

Elaine is very much at home in surroundings where men predominate. Attractive, dressed in colorful, fashionable clothes enhanced by discreet quantities of makeup, she is skilled in flirtation games and likes to engage in joking exchanges frequently spiced with sexual references. On one occasion she remarked to me that she would not want to live in a place where there were only women. Although she considered a few of the men "stinkers," she liked most of the male residents. One of her favorite recreational pastimes is to attend a local ballroom several blocks away. She loves to dance until the early hours and views this as a good form of exercise. One day when I met her in the hall, she confided that she had accepted a date from a man she met the night before. They had danced together all night and she had lied to him about her age. She was concerned that she knew so little about him, but he seemed so nice that she was going to take a chance. She then invited me up to her room to show me her evening gowns. On a rack next to the wall were at least a dozen dresses she had acquired over the years. Her favorite was a red one adorned with feathers and sequins. "Dancing makes me feel so good," she enthused; "I like a man to take me in his arms and waltz me around the floor." Men are an important part of her life, and their presence sustains her sense of femininity.

Overall, the personal histories of this chapter reflect among tenants of both sexes significant similarities in years of independent living, minimal involvement in social networks, and individualistic lifestyles. In contradistinction to conventional female roles, many of the women also maintain an ideology predicated on autonomy and self-reliance and demonstrate skill in the survival techniques of urban life. Most do not conform to stereotypic views of inner city women based on assumptions of social pathology but instead are pursuing patterns of daily living similar to those of their earlier years. These histories also support the reality of heterogeneity in lifestyles and social involvement among aged men and women living in the inner city (Cantor 1975; Sokolovsky and Cohen 1978).

Women as well as men in these surroundings are vulnerable to the negative consequences of health losses and similar crises because of limited social supports, personal disinclinations to use community services, and reluctance to enter into dependent relationships. In Chapter 5 I delve in greater detail into how living at the St. Regis makes possible access to assistance for both male and female residents in ways that are less threatening to the belief systems and ideologies that characterize this population.

Chapter 4

The World of Harold Willis

"I may be an independent, ornery cuss but I've always lived the way I wanted to." These words were spoken by Harold Willis, a seventy-four-year-old Caucasian man who lived in the St. Regis for four years. During the study, Harold became one of my most valued informants. As I came to know him more intimately, I developed a deep respect for the insightful quality of his observations. Through his eyes it is possible to perceive in intimate detail important aspects of collective living downtown from the viewpoint of an elderly person living there and to garner operationalized descriptions of behavioral norms governing significant areas of social interaction among the residents. Although idiosyncratic components are in evidence, Harold's personal history and perspectives on the quality of community life at the St. Regis are similar to those of other residents and illustrate a number of features of tenant interaction discussed in the foregoing chapters.

Over the years Harold has remained unmarried and has worked in a variety of skilled and semiskilled occupations. He maintains no contact with family members and has only a few friends on the outside that he occasionally visits. In his view, living with age peers is not a way of gaining new friends. He moved into the St. Regis primarily because of the cheap rent, the availability of assistance in time of need, and his desire to remain downtown for the convenience of services close by. He purposely avoids intimate involvement with other residents and prefers to see himself as a marginal participant in community affairs. His world view is essentially pragmatic and oriented toward the practical concerns of meeting daily living needs within his small income and following a round of daily activities in accustomed surroundings according to his personal preferences.

Harold grew up in Florida and by age fifteen was working full time for his father as a hod carrier in the construction business. He was an only child and both of his parents died while he was still a young man. Over the years he worked primarily in some phase of the building industry. Between periods of regular employment he rode the rails during the Depression, picked fruit in the central valleys of California, and was a labor agitator in the union struggles of the 1930s. Before his retirement five years earlier, he owned and operated a small construction business in Los Angeles. His varied work history and love of gambling were not conducive to the accumulation of savings, and he is now totally dependent on social security and veterans' benefits.

Although physically small, Harold has a sturdy, muscular build that would discourage anyone from "messing with him." He takes pride in his appearance and characteristically dresses in colorful casual clothes. A well-worn gray felt hat has been his close companion for years, and he is rarely seen without it. Although he mentions a mild heart condition, his general health is good and he pursues an active life. Much of his day he spends away from the St. Regis, deriving considerable pleasure from browsing in nearby discount stores or taking the bus to outlying areas of the city. Every few months he goes to Las Vegas to try out his luck at the gambling tables and to obtain relief for his sexual needs. He is proud of his gambling expertise and tells me he usually wins enough to pay for his expenses.

Harold has purposely avoided marital entanglement. The attendant responsibilities were not for him, although he has lived with several women in the past. He has few friends and wants to quietly live out the rest of his life according to his own dictates. "Tying yourself up with others only makes for trouble" is the theme permeating his views about forming close relationships with others. Four years ago he gave up his small apartment in Hollywood and moved to the St. Regis when he was no longer able to afford a car.

I first met Harold after I had been in the building for several months. The Arts and Crafts Club had decided on a project of building some window boxes for the main lobby which were to be filled with plants and placed in front of the bay windows overlooking the main street. Knowing of this plan, Charles Mason had already approached Harold to see if he would be interested in contributing some of his carpentering expertise. One day, as I turned the corner, Harold was waiting for me by the front door.

"Are you the lady who wants the boxes built?" he asked after introducing himself. "Maybe I can help you." After I expressed my appreciation for his interest, we proceeded to discuss the problem of finding a suitable location in which to make the boxes. Harold expressed his preference for a place to work where nosy tenants wouldn't be peering over his shoulder, explaining how in the past, if people bothered him, he would just walk off a job. We agreed that in the next few days I would try to find a suitable place.

After a number of phone calls I was able to obtain permission from a church several blocks away to use their workshop, where needed tools including an electric saw were available. I purchased some lumber and on an appointed day Harold helped me unload the materials from my car and carry them to the church basement. He was pleased with the prospect of the work ahead and made a few initial comments about how rusty his woodworking skills were. He tested the saw, put on a carpenter's apron that still carried a price tag, and proceeded to arrange the wood and make measurements. I didn't have to hang around, he told me, and could go attend to other business. On my return several hours later, he was just finishing the last of the four boxes and was obviously pleased with the results. I complimented him at length and together we took the finished items back to the St. Regis.

Later that same day Charles Mason dropped by my office and mentioned that it would be nice for me to find some suitable way to repay Harold for his efforts. When I suggested baking a cake, he felt that would be just right: "You know how fat Harold is. That means he loves his food; and besides, a cake is something you can give him without a lot of other people knowing about it."

Several days later I knocked on Harold's door, bearing a chocolate cake smothered in thick fudge icing. Evidently pleased, Harold said, "Now how did you know I would like something to eat? As if it isn't obvious by this," he added, patting a substantial expanse of stomach. As we sat down to share a piece of cake, he told me about two tenants he had spotted hanging around outside the church while he was building the boxes: "As if they didn't have anything better to do. That just shows you how nosy people are in this place."

As we talked further I shared with him some of my concerns about the complications involved in dealing with the social security office when tenants failed to receive their checks on time. He expressed considerable pessimism about the whole welfare system and explained that when anything went wrong with his checks, he had to deal with several places because he received more than one kind of pension. "When something goes wrong at least I'm healthy enough to go to the different offices and get things straightened out. But some of these poor people around here— they're too weak and sick to do anything, and so many of 'em just don't take care of it and put up with the consequences."

We turned to discussing the more general area of politics and Harold expressed a number of opinions about the Depression, the Roosevelt administration, and our current president. A socialist for years, he was bitterly critical of the exploitive character of our capitalist system. He was well versed in the writings of Marx and spoke knowledgeably about the Russian Revolution of 1917. He also talked about his labor union activities during the 1930s. "You may not think it now, but I was quite a guy in my day. I knew a lot of people who were really influential, and I could still get in touch with some of them if I wanted to. But all that's behind me now. I just want to keep out of things."

We talked too about the study I was doing. Harold expressed some skepticism about the possibility of writing about a group of people who were all so different, but he agreed to share some of his opinions with me as long as his real name was kept out of any written materials.

The next day Harold and I drove over to one of his favorite discount shopping areas to find some plastic plates suitable to go under the plants in the window boxes. As we wandered through several stores fingering household items, articles of clothing, and slightly damaged canned goods, Harold told me about the importance of stretching your dollars when you only had a certain amount of money coming in each month. It was necessary for him to shop carefully because he only had forty-five or fifty dollars a month to spend on food. "When I go to the check-out stand, they know when they see me that I only buy things on special. I keep on going to different stores until the price seems right. Why, I can buy a can of mackerel for thirty-nine cents that weighs sixteen ounces and a can of sardines for fifty-three cents that only weighs eight ounces. Maybe the mackerel doesn't taste as good, but the food value is better. And when you add some onions, tomatoes, and a few spices—it makes a good meal." With careful planning he could even make one chicken last for several days: "You can make a delicious soup from the wings and tail, and the rest you can fry and bake." He then made reference to spending habits developed over a lifetime of careful management: "You know, how careful I am is not just something I do because now I don't have much money. I've been like this all my life. When I worked at my trade, I could always get my materials cheaper than anybody else. When I grew up, you had to be careful." To obtain good bargains, however, it was necessary for him to cover considerable territory. He felt sorry for some of the tenants who were only able to walk to the corner store, where the prices were much higher.

In one store we selected some plates that appeared suitable for our needs, each one marked fifty-nine cents. As we were going through the cashier's stand, Harold asked if the marked price was the "fair" price or the discount price. The cashier called over the manager, who affirmed that the discount price was indeed fifty-nine cents. At this point Harold began to argue with him, stating that in other discount stores one price was visibly crossed out and a lower price written in. This had not been done on the plates we were purchasing. I could see that he was enjoying this kind of bargaining, but I was also beginning to feel embarrassed by all the fuss. I wasn't used to questioning pricing procedures. Harold turned to me and suggested we should go down the street and check out some of the other stores, but I argued against it, saying I was pressed for time. We ended up paying the fifty-nine cents, but as we were leaving, I felt that Harold was somehow displeased with me. I had interfered in a bargaining process that he enjoyed.

Two weeks later the Housing Authority sent over a dozen plants for the window boxes, and they had been temporarily deposited in the manager's office. Harold knew of this and was waiting for me outside my office. "Just the morning you'd pick to be late," he said somewhat impatiently. "Come on—let's get the plants and get the whole thing set up in the lobby. People around here have been waiting so long for these plants that they don't believe the damn things exist." When I said I still wanted to put another coat of varnish on the boxes, he exploded. "God, you women! Why do you always make things so complicated? I don't have the time to mess around like this. I'm going back to my room." Quickly I adopted a more conciliatory attitude. After some discussion he relented and we set up the boxes and plants as he directed. As we worked, several tenants paused to admire the results, one commenting that it had been a long time since she had seen begonias and that the touches of greenery made the lobby less like a funeral parlor.

A few weeks later Harold came down to the lobby while I was setting up for the monthly coffee party, both of my daughters, aged ten and fourteen, with me to help out. After I introduced him, he remarked on how pretty they were. Both giggled appropriately, and he added that they better watch out when the boys started coming around. I agreed.

Later that morning I asked Harold if he had ever had a family. He laughed and said he just wasn't the kind, "but I love kids and especially dogs." He told several stories illustrating how dogs always liked him and then returned to the subject of why he had never married. "I figured marriage wasn't for me. I wanted the freedom to go around and do things I wanted. Who needs all the problems that getting married can mean." When our talk was interrupted by several other tenants, Harold left and returned a short time later with a tiny ceramic animal for each of my daughters. It was just a present, he said, in return for being so nice and coming down to see everybody.

One day he invited me up to his room to show me his "tower of fancy" that he was in the process of constructing. The tower consisted of five delicately curved shelves made of bits and pieces of filigreed wood he retrieved from some trash bins behind an old warehouse. The unit was about twenty-four inches high and fastened to the wall above a small desk. He only wanted to place items on the shelves that had special significance for him. So far he had chosen a stuffed toy squirrel a friend had given him before he died. On top was a playful statue of a nude woman that he laughingly described as his imaginary girlfriend. I complimented him on his creation, and he went on to talk about the principles of design involved in putting the various pieces together.

Next Harold showed me an arrangement he had recently built around his stove. The backing consisted of several pieces of plywood that formed a large rectangle. In the center was a print of a country scene in which a small cottage was nestled under a grove of trees. Around the picture he had hung some measuring spoons, an egg beater, and a potato masher. "Some people looking at this picture would just see a shack surrounded by a bunch of bushes, but I don't. To me, when I see a picture like this, I think of places up in the mountains where they build those condominiums and tear down all the trees. I would never do that. I'd go to a place like this [indicating the picture] and build apartments that fit into the land and trees. In fact people would be able to drive by and not even know my building was there."

He continued to show me other significant areas in his room. Next to the stove was his work bench, a small table covered with several hammers, assorted screwdrivers, a saw, and small jars filled with a variety of screws and nails. Hanging from a nail on the wall was the carpenter's apron he had worn while making the window boxes. "Now when I sit here in this chair [pointing to a worn easy chair in the corner], I can sit and look at that ceramic cat over on the window sill and have a conversation with myself like "Who would make a cat that looked like that?" Then he pointed to his small eating table next to the stove. "Now, when I sit here and look at this picture [indicating a print on the wall of a barroom scene in the early West], I say to myself 'That's my club.' When I'm sitting here eating, I just imagine I'm there. And when I'm lying in bed, I can look at that picture of the ship over there [and here he pointed to a print of a schooner sailing rough seas] and lie back in bed and dream about traveling." He added that a personal dwelling should reflect the personalities of the occupants. When he entered his room he felt "at home."

Harold was now coming regularly to our Arts and Crafts Club. Although he declined to become involved in the activities, he often joined us for refreshments and sociable conversation. One day he dropped by to have his usual cup of coffee. Playfully he asked if we minded having "an unkempt, unshaven wino visiting for a while." I could see that this was his way of asking us to excuse the fact that he was unshaven. From this point the general talk assumed a joking flavor with sexual overtones, and Harold commented that his being there didn't necessarily mean that he wanted to make any time with us. We could trust him, he said, and his intentions were definitely honorable. "Anyway, I'm too old, so you have nothing to worry about."

One of the women in the group, who happened to live on Harold's floor, commented that he was a quiet neighbor and never seemed to have any wild parties. "Oh yes I do," Harold responded. "But no one knows about them because I make sure my guests are quiet. Now, when I want my women to come in, I just have them go up on the roof and climb down into my apartment on a rope. But this one day this girl was climbing down and the rope broke. She got so mad she never came to see me anymore." Everyone laughed appropriately, although I couldn't honestly see what was so funny.

Judy Cummings, who had the reputation of being a flirt, was present during this conversation and came over to Harold, wiggling her hips suggestively. She said when she was young she really knew how to have a good time and he had better watch his step with her. Both were enjoying the flirtatious quality of these remarks, and Harold again assured us that he was past his prime. Everyone laughed and Judy said she would just have to find her action somewhere else. By this time the class had ended and after the materials were put away, we slowly dispersed and went on to other affairs.

In the months that followed, Harold and I became good friends. By now I genuinely liked this interesting and highly verbal man, but in all honesty, I sometimes had a sinking feeling when I saw him coming, knowing that he was good for at least several hours of nonstop conversation. As trust and rapport increased between us, he shared his opinions about his personal philosophy and his attitudes toward other tenants.

One day we were sitting in his room sharing a bottle of beer. (Whenever I visited him I noticed that he was always careful to leave his door partly open. He wanted to do this because he disliked the idea of other tenants gossiping about our relationship.) Harold began to share personal reflections.

He felt he had lived well and had done just about everything. All during his life no one could tell him what to do; he always did what he wanted, in his own way. Now his preference was to be alone in a place where not too many people knew him or anything about his background. He only wanted peace and quiet. "But you know, in all the things I've done, everybody—even my enemies —respected me. I never did anything that wasn't honest, and I never backed down from what I did either. And I've never done anything I was ashamed of. Sure I spent several years in the penitentiary, but I didn't regret that either. And I'm not afraid to die. Hell, it happens to us all sooner or later, and I'm ready to go when my time comes. When you reach this time of life, it becomes a matter of acceptance of things as they are."

Harold was of the opinion that a lot of the people in the building felt as he did. "The fact that you're now old—that you can't even earn any more money—means that you just have to take the income you have and make the best of it. You have to stretch your pennies and become a good shopper. If cooking in your room means you stretch out your monthly check further—then you do it. To me, growing old successfully is a matter of making the best deal you can with what's available to you."

To illustrate what he was talking about, he described the life-style of one of his neighbors:

Now this old guy is eighty-three and he's busy all the time. He goes down to the produce market and walks all the way. It's about two miles from here. He goes down about five in the morning, and when he gets there, he collects all the vegetables that are left lying around. He's a vegetarian. Every day he comes back here with a basketful of everything he can find. The other day he showed me this old piece of carpet he found in a garbage can. He scrubbed it clean and said he was going to use it as a mat beside his bed. Now that kind of person is getting what he can out of life. He's a professional scrounger. And he's always into something. You know he even has enough food left over to feed a pack of dogs somewhere around here.

He went on to tell me about his recent trip to Las Vegas. He had been a heavy gambler most of his life, and for a short time had worked as a dealer in Las Vegas, where he maintained some people still remember him. He preferred, he said, to go by himself because then he didn't have to worry about what a bunch of other people wanted to do. Thus, he would never go on the bus tours popular with some residents. "Hell, I'm never lonely there." On his last trip, the manager of the hotel found out it was his birthday. A cake was sent over to him, and for the rest of the night drinks were free.

Years ago, when he had more money, he really made some killings, but now he had to bet more conservatively. Someday soon, though, he was going to get together a stake and make a lot of money to finance an invention he had in mind. He wanted to win enough money to design and build an electric car because he was fed up with the way those "goddam oil companies were ruining

the country with the high price of gas and all the oil shortages."
But these kinds of plans took money, and going to Las Vegas was
the surest way of getting it. A week later I ran into Harold in the
lobby and he stopped just long enough to tell me that he had decided to scrap his project about the electric car. He just read in
the paper that someone had received from the federal government
a grant for several hundred thousand dollars to develop one—so
why should he bother.

On one occasion Harold agreed to take me on a walking tour of
the surrounding area to point out some features he felt were important to other residents. First of all he cited the proximity of
the bus stops to the St. Regis. Being able to ride the buses con-
veniently was, he felt, crucial to most older people and enabled
them to save money. "Hell, some people will go as far as Pasa-
dena if they think they can get a good bargain." Pointing to a
cotton shirt displayed in the window of a discount store we were
passing, he added, "Now, I know where I could go in Hollywood
and get a shirt like that for a couple of dollars less."

Within several blocks of the St. Regis, Harold pointed out a
large market, a liquor store, and various small shops where items
ranging from can openers to used clothing could be obtained
at reasonable prices. In his view, the older population of the
downtown area was essential to the economic well-being of these
smaller stores. "Now what do you think would happen to all
these old hotels, restaurants, and stores if the old people didn't
live here? Each month when the food stamps are issued, these
stores are loaded with everybody buying everything they can lay
their hands on. If you took away the food stamp program and
moved a lot of these old age pensioners out of the area, a lot of
these places would go broke. That's why the politicians let the
old people stay here." I mentioned that many of the residents
seemed to have lived in the area for quite a few years. He agreed
and added, "A lot of the people down here wouldn't like it anywhere else. They're familiar with how things are."

By this time we had arrived back at the St. Regis and continued our conversation in a quiet corner of the downstairs lounge.

Harold talked further about some of the reasons why residents remain in the building. He considered the name "St. Regis" nothing but a fancy title for an old people's home. "People who live here just know they are sitting around waiting to die. They don't have anywhere else they can go. The only difference between this place and an old man's home is that in those places, you don't have to pay anything. Here you have to pay the Housing Authority for rent, and then the government pays you with a social security check." He smiled and added, "Now does that really make sense? This place here is really run by the federal government you know. So they give it to us in one way and take it away in another."

He likened some features of life at the St. Regis to what you would find in institutional settings. For instance, going up in the elevator at night after the front door was locked, you would often hear the remark that it was lock-up time. When I asked if this phrase referred only to the fact that the front door was being locked, he smiled and said, "No, honey-bunch. They're using that word just the same as you would in an institution or a prison. Maybe a lot of the people living here don't exactly think of it that way, but that's what they mean. They go up to their rooms and lock themselves in. And a lot of them don't go out on the streets after six at night. Now that's really being locked up, even if you do it yourself."

A little later he spoke about the matter-of-fact way in which death and illness are regarded in this setting. "When you're sitting around and some person is being carried out on a stretcher —you don't hear people being worried about who it is. People just go about their everyday business. And it would be a dumb thing to ask the person lying on the stretcher how they are feeling. Obviously they aren't feeling well because why would they be leaving like that in the first place?" He laughed at this piece of ironic humor.

Harold turned, then, to styles of interaction with other residents and how they are more realistically oriented than you would find in other places. For example, it would be silly to ask people sitting around the lobby about their health. Maybe expressions of

concern fitted the world that a person like myself came from, but
these kinds of comments were out of place in his surroundings.
To my query about how residents did usually greet each other,
he responded:

> Well, you ask questions that mean something, like Has the
> mailman come? or Are those goddam elevators working to-
> day? These are the kinds of questions you can say to anyone
> who happens to be standing around. Now maybe some
> people won't answer back, or if they feel like it, maybe
> they'll say something. But the last thing I would do would
> be go into the lobby and ask somebody about their health.
> They may be feeling awful and that's the last thing they
> want to be reminded of—let alone talk about. Besides,
> most of them feel you don't really care about their health
> anyway. At least most people in this place are honest with
> each other. Now if someone did you dirt, you would just
> tell them where to go. The thing is not to be a phony.
> That's the way to get along with people who live here.

At this point another resident came over to say hello, and Harold, who disliked sharing our conversations with other tenants,
quickly announced that he had to go to the market and left.

A few months later, while we were sitting over a cup of coffee
in a restaurant, Harold shared more of his impressions of other
tenants and their lifestyles. He felt that the population could be
divided into at least four or five types:

> There are the possessors. These are people who figure they
> know all the ropes and act as if they own the place. Then
> comes the elite—these guys think they're better than any-
> one else. Next come the gentle guys, and they go around
> trying to please everybody. And then come the ones who
> keep to themselves all the time. These guys you hardly ever
> see and a lot of them stay drunk all the time. Drinking isn't
> something these guys started when they retired. They've
> been drinking for years, and some you never see. They stay

in their rooms and only come out when they need booze
or food.

I asked if there were any professional hustlers among the residents. He laughed and said, "Honey—you meet hustlers in
every walk of life." Talking about his own experiences, he explained that the ability to get money out of people sometimes
made the difference between starving or making it during the Depression. But he didn't feel that much real hustling went on now
in the building. "Sure, some of the people here have been hustlers
in their time. But now they're sitting back resting on their lau-
rels and enjoying life. They get government money to make it on
now, so why should they bother?"

On another occasion shortly afterward Harold and I were sitting in the same restaurant when I expressed an interest in knowing more about the relationships between some of the men and
women in the building. This topic was obviously meaningful to
him and he spoke at some length:

> Now take one lady who used to live here. She used to sit
> with the men all the time in the lobby, and I know some of
> them could get some action from her if they put up the
> money. But most of these guys like to get it outside. Not
> that some there don't have affairs going on. You know, a
> woman who used to live next door to me—she used to cook
> for some guy across the hall. Sometimes I'd see them com-
> ing out of his room and I figured something was going on.
> But I'm not one to say anything about things like that. But
> usually the guys here stay away from the women because of
> the gossip. Now take you and me. Don't think there hasn't
> been some talk when people see us together. But I figure it's
> alright because you're an outsider. You don't have to live
> here so the gossip can't do you any harm.

As we talked generally about the subject of sex and older
people, Harold expressed his feelings in this way: "I never got
married but the fact that I'm old doesn't mean I don't have any

sex drives. I still do—that hasn't changed. And I've been with a lot of women in my time and I've really loved some of them too. But sometimes I get up and look in the mirror at my body and think, 'God, is this the body of a man?' When you get old like this, you become something else. I guess it must be just as hard for a woman too. I mean, she has to feel the same way." He referred as well to the double standard in which sex is usually more available for men than women:

These guys, they work, they retire, they finally come here. Their life hasn't changed much. They can still get the kind of sex they need on the side. The women though—Can you picture an old lady going to Las Vegas and getting the kind of action I do? Last time I went there, four girls approached me, and I finally went with one who would turn a trick for twenty-five dollars. Women need sex just as much, but when you get to be that old, what guy is going to look at them? Some of the women here, I guess, are still good looking—sort of—but then the guys usually want the younger ones anyway.

Redirecting the conversation, Harold again demonstrated the kind of sensitivity that made me respect his opinions so highly. He was aware of the kind of study I was trying to do but cautioned against lumping people into one category. Even in the things he had just been talking about, there were lots of exceptions, and he felt that one of the problems in our society is that we classify too much.

Now you take the people here in this place. Everybody's different. And even though we've been talking about the way the guys and women get along, you'll find some who need men and some who can't stand them. You find some who are stand-offish and some who couldn't care less. You just can't talk about a thing and then assume that everybody does it in the same way. Whether or not these people here sit around gossiping in the lobby or stay in their rooms all the time or are gone most of the day—still, they're living out their lives in the same way they've probably lived for years. People don't change just because they get old.

Chapter 5

Helping One Another

"You have to be able to look after yourself around here. People who live in this place are only concerned about themselves," Charles Baron observed on one occasion among friends in the Minority Circle. Many tenants repeatedly assert that others are primarily occupied with self-oriented matters and exhibit little concern about the needs of others. Initially, I assumed that a scarcity of personal resources combined with patterns of reclusive, independent living accounted for this apparent focus on self. As the time I was in the setting increased, though, so did my awareness of the many types of helping behavior people quietly entered into. Gradually I came to understand that these activities constituted one of the most important features of community life.

Some tenants shopped and prepared meals for those who were ill; a few altered clothes or mended garments for men who were not adept with needle and thread; several men fixed small electrical appliances. Others performed favors such as bringing back food bargains from more distant stores. One woman related to me how she helped an unlikeable neighbor suffering from lung cancer. She had little liking for him and regarded him as an unpleasant person who rarely spoke to anyone. One night when he was suffering from a severe attack of pain, he knocked on her door and asked if she would help him get to the hospital.

I felt so sorry for him. He said he was afraid to go back to the hospital because if he did, he was going to die. I helped him call a taxi and went along with him. They kept us waiting in the examining room for two hours before the doctor finally came in. The man was frightened and started to cry. I put my arm around him and tried to make him feel better but he kept saying over and over—"I'm going to die—I'm going to die." He was finally admitted and I went back to visit him almost every day. Sometimes he wasn't very nice to me and said things that weren't very kind. But I kept on going back anyway because there didn't seem to be anyone else to visit him. He died in about two weeks and I wrote to his sister in the East about it. He'd asked me to do that. It's so sad when you're all alone like that. If I got that sick and had no one to help, I hope someone would do the same for me.

I also observed the frequency in which some form of payment was involved. One tenant tried to persuade me to accept several dollars when I obtained a reduction in his medical bill. In spite of my protests, he finally insisted on settling the debt by giving me a pair of well-worn pants he thought could be made over to fit one of my children. Soon I came to appreciate that many attached considerable importance to the act of repayment, and I found myself taking home a variety of goods such as handmade potholders, baked cookies, decorative jars, and containers of homemade soup. One man took the time to adjust an electric stove for his nearsighted neighbor and was rewarded with a bottle of beer; another helped a woman find a missing apartment key and was given a dollar for his efforts. When a seventy-six-year-old woman returned from the hospital after a severe heart attack, another resident living on the same floor prepared her meals. Several months earlier their positions had been reversed. Motivations for assisting, too, were often openly expressed in terms of expected returns at some future date, should the need arise, or in relation to repaying someone for similar help received in the past. Of course altruistic concerns were influential, but in this setting the frequency of helping seemed to arise primarily from utilitarian concerns in that such acts increased the likelihood of receiving similar aid in return.

Formal on-site services such as medical assistance and planned meals are not available in the St. Regis, and many tenants are disinclined to use outside community agencies.[1] In addition to a sense of disillusionment about the effectiveness of publicly sponsored aid programs, which is based on years of exposure to inexplicable government forms, confusing referrals, and complex eligibility requirements, asking for aid from outside sources can also be antithetical to deeply held beliefs about the negative implications for self that receiving charity implies. Therefore the availability of informal support systems within the building becomes an essential determinant of ability to retain an independent status in familiar surroundings.

Given the reality of extensive needs, what kinds of informal support systems are available to the tenants and how effective are these helping networks in the prevention of premature institutionalization? As friendly ties do not appear to provide the basis for reciprocal aid, what are the value systems affecting the ways in which these transactions occur?

Theoretical Perspectives on Assistance

Lopata (1975) effectively defines support systems as "the giving and receiving of objects, services, social and emotional supports defined by the receiver and the giver as necessary or at least helpful in maintaining a style of life" (35). These systems can be further differentiated into (a) primary (informal) relations involving mutual exchanges between family, friends, and other familiars and (b) secondary (formal) systems in which transactions are more depersonalized and consist of aid made available through community agencies and official caregivers (Lopata 1975).

Because of limited family ties, poverty, poor health, and reclusive ways of life, the urban elderly have been identified as a high-risk group for assistance needs (Shapiro 1971). For example, Ehrlich (1976) and Stephens (1976) found that SRO hotel dwellers frequently strived to retain their independence in ways that adversely affected their well-being. Other findings, however,

challenged assumptions of social isolation and found that interpersonal linkages among aged people in the inner city were
more complex and extensive than originally conceived.

In their studies of social networks among elderly residents in
Manhattan SRO hotels, Cohen and Sokolovsky (1980) discovered
that although many were relatively isolated compared with other
urban samples, only 2 percent had no personal contacts and 94
percent had multiplex linkages. Yet in the range of transactions
that occurred—providing money, alcoholic beverages, food,
medical help; giving advice; and social visitation—intimate
ties were rarely involved. The researchers concluded that the
utilitarian nature of these activities limited personal involvement in ways that were congruent with established values of
autonomy and self-reliance. Contacts were primarily activated
in time of need and functioned to reduce reliance on institutional-
ized supports.

In spite of the fact that SRO hotels often function as halfway
stations between independent and dependent living because they
provide access to assistance from staff and other residents (Erickson and Eckert 1977), elderly tenants remain vulnerable to unwanted institutionalization when their functioning capacities decline. In their uncertain world, urban redevelopment, transient
populations, and death or illness of significant others can undermine the dependability of existing networks. These buildings
contain disproportionate numbers of physically impaired elderly
compared with national samples of age peers (Bild and Havighurst 1976; Eckert 1979b) and other living alternatives at
affordable prices are scarce. When illness strikes and reliable acquaintances or neighbors are no longer available, unwanted institutionalization may be the only recourse.

Age-segregated housing appears to be a viable alternative.
Studies of retirement communities reveal that living in age-dense
settings results in the development of mutual aid systems that
function to supplement weak family resources and declining capacities (Jonas and Wellin 1981). For example, in a comprehensive examination of the relation between varying residential concentrations of aged people and the degree of involvment in local

group life, Rosow (1967) discovered that those living alone in age-dense settings were twice as likely to receive help from neighbors during times of illness than single elderly people residing in age-dispersed settings. He also found that single aged persons in age-concentrated buildings expressed less concern about the availability of help. Similarly, a group of elderly widows living in a public housing project in San Franisco evidenced widely spread patterns of mutual assistance such as providing care during illness and remaining alert to the possibility of crisis events such as accidents or death (Hochschild 1973).[2] Physical proximity and age homogeneity then become important variables that not only function to enhance friendship ties but also increase the availability of help and promote the existence of comforting beliefs about the opportunities for receiving aid in case of need.

Availability, rather than the numerical frequency, of assistance transactions has greater relevance in assessing the advantages of age-dense living. E. S. Sherman (1975a) examined mutual assistance patterns between aged people living in various age-segregated settings and their neighbors and children. It was found that residents of an apartment tower and a downtown retirement hotel had limited family ties and exhibited fewer instances of neighborly help than occupants of other types of housing. A closer examination of the findings revealed that family relationships rather than the kind of housing were important factors in accounting for these differences. Referring to the "cumulative effect of interdependency," the researcher surmised that those who were used to relying on their children in time of need could more easily turn to their neighbors than those who were accustomed to long-term patterns of autonomy and self-reliance. Lifestyles rather than the type of housing were more likely to determine the actual frequency of helping transactions.[3]

Thus investigations of the viability of collective living for elderly people in urban settings should more realistically focus on both form and structure of supportive networks as well as the ways in which lifelong habits affect use patterns. In addition, attention should be given to the cultural rules affecting the nature of these exchanges in community settings (Wentowski 1981) and how these rules are situationally interpreted according to differing perceptions of need.

Status Similarities

Requesting and receiving assistance from similar others can be less threatening to individual perceptions of continuing competence and self-esteem.[4] According to Festinger's (1954) theory of social comparisons, we tend to select those whose circumstances are more nearly like our own as a basis for comparison. The implication here is that greater similarities in capacities and circumstances reduce the possibilities of uncomfortable contrasts that can have negative implications for self. The acknowledgment of inferiority can be the cost of receiving assistance from those who occupy positions of greater status and power (Dowd 1980).

Age similarities may also contribute to the availability of assistance. A prolonged illness, the death of a helping friend, reduced locomotive capacities, and the serious consquences of accidental falls are age-related problems with which most elderly are familiar. Indeed, research studies have substantiated noticeable increments in helping behavior among those faced with the necessity of coping with common threats in both naturally occurring crises and experimentally induced situations (Lanzetta 1958; Midlarsky 1971; Sherif et al. 1961).

The extent to which these kinds of concerns are shared would understandably be less in age-dispersed settings where everyday matters are more likely to be centered around familial and occupational affairs. But in settings where aged people live singly and where critical events involving death and illness happen frequently, a consciousness of kind predominates in which individual perceptions of need assume a collective character. This shared awareness increases the possibilities of discovery, should crises occur, through greater alertness to signs of trouble, such as an unanswered telephone or uncollected mail.

The Instrumental Character of Assistance Exchanges

Societal norms usually de-emphasize the utilitarian aspects of helping behavior but for economically marginal aged people faced with declining material and physical resources, altruism becomes a luxurious commodity few can afford. Surviving in a demanding urban world when personal capacities are becoming increasingly limited necessitates anticipated benefits of some kind when help is extended to others. For example, in her study of an SRO hotel in downtown Detroit, Stephens (1976) found that relationships among the elderly tenants were primarily instrumental in character, which was "understandable in face of the constant need to mobilize extremely limited resources to maintain living conditions in an antagonistic environment" (16). Maintenance of self was the fundamental concern of these "tough survivors" who showed little concern toward the misfortunes of those sharing the same living space. Social relationships were limited at best, with each person behaving in ways deemed profitable to his or her own individual needs and interests.

It is difficult to imagine, however, any grouping, regardless of the degree of social and material deprivation, that is totally lacking in altruistic behavior of some kind. In a definitive article exploring factors affecting helping and altruism, Berkowitz (1972) argues that at least some forms of helping are influenced by norms of social responsibility and feelings of empathy. But he additionally states that prospects of external rewards are probably the major determinants of such behavior and also that members of groupings in which social relations are distant are more inclined toward reciprocity perspectives.

The reciprocal nature of assistance exchanges can also be viewed as contributing to the stability of social interaction in a community where intragroup relations are fragmented and characterized by dissension and mistrust. Reciprocal norms can function to regulate exchange patterns and inhibit the development of exploitive relations that could be disruptive (Gouldner 1966). When personal relations are uncertain among people living in close proximity, helping behavior that is based on the giving and receiving of equivalent aid can safely bypass the building of personal obligations that could lead to unwanted personal involvement and can contribute to social stability by minimizing the possibilities of taking advantage (Suttles and Street 1970). Under these conditions, the reciprocity principle operates as a substitute for the lack of interpersonal trust and also functions to guarantee the replenishment of scarce assets. Equivalence of exchange thus becomes a mechanism that preserves private lifestyles and makes assistance transactions more acceptable to those more accustomed to solitary ways. Horizontal exchanges among status equals involving expectations of repayment not only are congruent with important values of autonomy and a dislike for indebtedness but also result in the creation of a more reliable network of relationships.[5]

The reciprocal nature of assistance patterns in materially deprived settings can also be profitably viewed in relation to the theory of social exchange. Simmel (1950) states that "all contacts between men rest on the scheme of giving and returning the equivalence" (87). Exchange theory as developed by Homans (1958) and Blau (1964) is grounded in these same kinds of concerns. Their contention is that human conduct is primarily of an instrumental character in which both parties to the transaction will attempt to maximize benefits and reduce perceived costs in the furtherance of particularistic goals.[6] This essentially rational interpretation of human behavior assumes that individuals will persist in social encounters that continue to provide valued rewards that exceed perceived penalties.

Although exchange theory does not account for all of the factors affecting motivations to provide assistance, its postulates can be meaningfully utilized at the St. Regis to highlight some of the situational determinants of availability of help and the importance of a balance-of-payments principle among tenants. Under conditions of scarcity in both personal and material resources, tenants are more than usually exposed to the emergence of exploitive relations that could be socially disruptive in a setting where concerns for equality function to guarantee a more equitable distribution of available resources.

Many in the building can be characterized as marginal survivors. Former low-earning capacities, personality dispositions, and life circumstances have undermined their ability to accumulate surplus resources to cushion the needs of old age. Norms of repayment thus enable them to preserve a sense of equivalence and to reduce the instances of unfair advantage. Operating according to exchange principles whereby members reciprocate with actions of similar value enhances their ability to ask for and receive help under conditions less threatening to their limited resources and perceptions of independence.

Outside Assistance

Many residents dislike using community services and will do so only when there is no other alternative. A small percentage go to nearby nutrition sites, but many prefer to eat in restaurants or prepare meals in their own rooms. Some, in cases of medical disability, obtain housekeeping assistance grants from the Department of Public Social Services to hire someone to perform cleaning chores, but others use their own funds because they dislike complying with complicated eligibility requirements. I did not come across one instance in which, in times of financial crisis, a resident applied to a community agency for emergency financial aid. Money is either borrowed from friends or other tenants and repaid when monthly pension checks arrive.

The greatest reliance on outside services is to meet medical needs. Many tenants have their own private doctors; other regularly attend clinics at county medical facilities and several nearby private hospitals. Visiting nurses are often in the building, and in emergency situations a medical rescue team will be on the premises within half an hour. Still a number of tenants resist seeking needed medical care because they dislike doctors or fear attracting official attention to increasing frailty. Many prefer to rely on home remedies and patent medicines, believing that old fashioned cures are more effective. One man instructed me in the capacity of paprika to help prevent colds, lung congestion, stomach problems, and constipation. Garlic, considered another potent cure-all, not only was supposedly effective against flu and some communicable diseases but also helped to increase sexual potency. And other tenants place their faith in the healing powers of God.

Family members are infrequently involved when help is needed.[7] In situations of sudden illness or chronic disability, I observed few instances in which a son or daughter cared for an ailing parent. There were, however, some situations in which residents moved in with immediate relatives during extended illnesses. In the following example, Clara Barstow describes the circumstances under which one male tenant who had been ill for several months went to live with his sister in Arizona: "He was so sick he didn't know where he was half the time, so I called his sister in Arizona and she told me to send him there by bus." Several days later Clara helped him pack, called a taxi, and sent the man down to the Greyhound Bus depot. In a few hours she began thinking that he might have caught the wrong bus and asked another tenant who was a good friend of hers to go down and check. "And it's a good thing I did that. When my friend got there he found this poor guy wandering around not knowing what to do. So he put him on the right bus and I sure hope he got to Phoenix O.K. Maybe sometime I should call his sister to find out what happened, but phone calls like that are expensive."

For many tenants, assistance is generally unavailable from family members because of estranged relations, lack of sustained contact over many years, distance, or personal preference. Thus significant numbers must rely on support systems existing in their place of residence.

Staff and Available Help

In addition to their regular duties, staff members informally provide supportive services that effectively supplement the diminishing capacities of some tenants. Other studies of the aged living in SRO hotels also find that hotel employees constitute an important source of assistance. Residents of downtown San Diego hotels, for example, frequently relied on hotel employees for running errands, maintenance repairs, and moving heavy objects (Erickson and Eckert 1977). In privately owned facilities, however, the availability of staff assistance may be less reliable than it is in residential complexes operated by government agencies and religious organizations. Stephens (1976) described the rapid turnover of some employees in an SRO hotel in Detroit and found that relations between the manager and residents on the granting of special favors and services were capricious and often based on profit-oriented considerations.[8] Although management personnel and employees in publicly subsidized buildings can be deficient in their caretaking responsibilities (Francis 1981), their performance is still regulated to a greater extent by the necessity of adhering to guidelines established by outside regulatory bodies. Public employees also enjoy higher salaries, benefit packages, and opportunities for advancement based on performance than do hired personnel in SRO hotels catering to low-income people. These employment circumstances increase the reliability of staff assistance by reducing employee turnover and providing the impetus to assume additional responsibilities for the welfare of tenants.

At the St. Regis, the manager provides a number of helping services that are beyond formally defined administrative duties. She will often request the security guard to conduct periodic checks through the night when a tenant is known to be seriously ill. In the event of sudden sickness or death, she attempts to locate family members. When a tenant unaccountably disappears, she will spend hours checking hospitals, emergency clinics, and police stations. She will also assist in contacting needed community agencies upon request, encourage residents to participate in nearby recreational programs, deliver messages from concerned relatives, and on occasion give advice about personal problems. In these services she views herself somewhat as a surrogate parent: "In lots of ways the people around here are like grown children and we have to take care of them."

The security guards also engage in a number of assistance activities in addition to their protective functions (Table 1.1). During the night they will assist inebriated tenants to their rooms and open apartment doors when keys are missing. One guard in particular makes himself available to exchange friendly comments with some who are lonely and in need of comforting talk. When a tenant is suspiciously absent from public view, other tenants will frequently ask the guard to check the missing person's apartment, and such timely intervention has averted serious consequences. A woman who had fallen and broken her hip in the bathroom was discovered within a few hours, and another resident was taken to the hospital in time following a serious heart attack in his room.

Before his untimely demise, the custodian provided important care for some incapacitated tenants. On one occasion when I was sitting outside the manager's office Jesus came by dragging an arsenal of mops, brooms, and buckets. As we talked I asked him what happened in case of an emergency when the main office was closed.[9] He smiled and replied, "Oh, I often take care of it. I call the ambulance if the person wants me to." We then spoke about his other caretaking activities. Presently he was looking after four people who were sick and "all alone in the world." In return for a small fee, he was buying their food and tidying their apartments on a daily basis. He also did general housecleaning for others who preferred not to be involved in rigorous cleaning chores. For a ten-dollar bill he was available to shampoo rugs, wash walls, scrub stoves, and clean bathrooms. "Now take Mr. Livingston," he said. "He can hardly walk. I help him down to the lobby each day, wash and iron his clothes, and get him breakfast from across the street. Sometimes I think I have too much to do. But you know some of these old people find it hard to trust anybody— but they know me and like me."

Many expressed affection for this man, but some also felt he made substantial sums of money from those who had few alternatives. At the time of his death, his loss was deeply felt and residents personally contributed approximately two hundred dollars to send his body back to Mexico. As one tenant said, "I don't know how some of the people around here will get along without him."[10]

Tenants, it is interesting to note, give little public recognition to the many sevices staff members informally provide. These additional helping activities have a taken-for-granted character, and expressions of criticism are more likely to be heard than appreciation. These attitudes indicate basic differences in expectations between tenants and management about the kinds of services that should be available.

On a formal level, management views the St. Regis essentially as an apartment building where the occupants are supposed to be largely responsible for their own needs. But residents have at least two different points of view on the matter. Many lived before in private hotels and were accustomed to regular linen changes and rooms being periodically cleaned. Others feel that in spite of low rentals, additional services such as housecleaning assistance during illness should be an expected structural feature in a retirement facility. Thus residents view helping acts performed by staff members as often inadequate in relation to their expectations about what should be provided in a place defined both as a government facility and a "hotel."

Critical attitudes toward Housing Authority employees are functional in several ways. Residents who are dependent on staff for assistance can view their declining abilities in less threatening ways. When help received from staff members can be redefined in terms of services to which tenants are justly entitled, perceptions of self-competence are not undermined and help can be accepted without feelings of indebtedness or incompetence. In addition, finding fault with the ways in which staff members perform has a leveling effect that cognitively reduces status differences in a setting where considerable power lies in the hands of official gatekeepers and where residents are unable to exercise much control over bureaucratic policies.

Intratenant Helpfulness

Although assistance from staff members is a valuable resource for some tenants, most prefer to turn to one another in time of need. In these transactions, abiding by principles of equivalence is the preferred mode for many who wish to avoid personal indebtedness and pay their own way. These transactions usually involve borrowing and lending money, exchanging goods and services, providing household assistance during prolonged illness, or helping in crises, which can involve medical emergencies and possible death.

Financial Exchanges

Money is a scarce commodity when most depend solely on limited old-age benefits arriving at the beginning of every month. Unforeseen medical expenses, unlucky bets at the racetrack, and inflationary prices for food and clothing consume limited funds in unanticipated ways when cash reserves are minimal. Being able to borrow a few dollars during such times allows at least the purchase of enough food to last until check day. Participants in money exchanges are not necessarily obligated by ties of friendship. Stringent repayment rules operate, and negative sanctions are levied against those who violate them. One man describes the normative expectations surrounding money transactions in this way:

> I could go into the lobby any day of the week and ask for a loan. As a matter of fact, I bought something last Sunday that left me a little short. I went up to this guy in the lobby — he wasn't a particular friend of mine — but he seemed to be the only one around. I told him I was a little tap city right now and would he lend me a little change. This guy — I didn't know his name — lent me a couple dollars and asked if I wanted more. I said no and thanked him. But don't get me wrong. That wasn't a gift. You always have to pay the money back. If you don't you get to be known as a bum.

In situations where money is not repaid, criticism directed against the offender can transcend considerations of sex and financial need. One woman who was injured during a robbery borrowed twenty-five dollars from another resident with the promise she would repay the loan when her social security arrived in several weeks. Two months went by and she failed to make restitution. She was subsequently bad-mouthed around the building, and the degree of criticism was so intense that she became to all intents and purposes a social outcast. Even the eventual repayment of the loan at a later date did little to restore her reputation.

Such reactions may seem extreme, but under conditions of scarcity the misuse of borrowing privileges can jeopardize the willingness of others to lend—an important recourse when monthly incomes average around $315 and pension checks only arrive on a monthly basis.

Common residence also limits the risk involved in making loans and operates as a type of security against the possibilities of default. Individual instances of borrowing quickly become a matter of public knowledge, and acts of repayment are carefully noted. It is also difficult for debtors to avoid contact with lenders when mail must be picked up and the lobby regulars carefully scrutinize those entering and leaving the building.

In isolated instances, however, involving extreme hardship and a recipient judged as mentally incompetent, loans can be made altruistically without expectation of repayment. For example, Mabel Evans, a tiny unprepossessing woman who was regarded as somewhat senile because of her forgetfulness and confused conversation, became seriously ill and was transferred to a convalescent home. When I called to find out how she was getting along, a nurse informed me that she had run away several days ago. A few weeks later as I was entering the lobby, Charles Mason called me over and related this story: "You know that little lady—the one you were always seeing? Well she wandered in here a couple of days ago looking for a place to stay. It was raining outside and we knew there weren't any rooms here. So one of the guys here took her over to the hotel across the street and got her a room for a couple of days. She didn't have any money, so he paid thirty dollars out of his own pocket. That's money he won't ever see again. She's confused, you know, a person like that shouldn't be loose wandering around."

During the conversation the man who had been Mabel's benefactor was sitting next to Mr. Mason. He added that he didn't really care about getting the money back. "Hell, I'd help out a dog in weather like that. Besides, she's a nice little lady and we all felt sorry for her." Several weeks later Mr. Mason informed me that Mabel had returned and repaid the loan.

Goods and Services

Residents commonly exchange a variety of goods, services, and favors related to the necessities of routine living. These transactions include swapping household items such as furniture and kitchen utensils, selling used clothing, running errands, shopping for bargain items at the market, giving away left-over food, getting the mail, hanging freshly laundered curtains, picking up cleaning, and repairing household appliances. In many of these activities the principle of reciprocity is carefully maintained.

Exchanging material goods frequently involves cash payments or swapping items of comparable worth. One man describes how his neighbor insisted on paying him for the use of a portable electric stove to replace one that had been taken out for repairs:

This funny old coot who lives right across from me—I don't know him very well because he keeps to himself a lot. But he told me he didn't have anything to cook on. So I told him he could just borrow this two-burner electric stove of mine. I paid nineteen dollars for it four years ago and never used it. But the old guy said he wouldn't take it unless he could give me money for it. He took out his wallet and peeled off nineteen dollars. I could see he only had one dollar left, so I said, "Hey, you're going to be short. Just give me ten dollars now and pay me the rest later." But he said no—that a dollar was plenty for him to live on. So I took the money. He felt better doing it that way.

Another woman who was moving out gave her neighbor some framed prints that were too bulky to fit into packing boxes. Before she left, he reciprocated by giving her a box full of used paperbacks. Telling me about the incident, she sighed and said, "I didn't really want any more stuff to take, but he was so insistent I couldn't refuse. He's a nice old man and I didn't want to hurt his feelings."

For some tenants, providing services for money is an additional source of income and reaffirms former occupational identity in satisfying ways. One woman who worked in a tailoring shop for twenty years before retiring regularly mends and alters clothing for several men in return for a small fee. She told me that when she left her trade at the age of sixty-two because of a heart condition, she swore she would never touch a needle and thread again. Yet here she is, doing favors for "some of the nice men around here for a few dollars." Another tiny, dark-haired woman, still vigorous in her middle seventies, was formerly a housekeeper for a wealthy family. She is sometimes available to clean apartments and in addition mends and irons clothing. A former bookkeeper interprets complicated government forms, and a retired electrician repairs television sets and small appliances at minimal cost. Performing these services provides a continuing sense of usefulness, while their availability at bargain prices extends the purchasing power of limited incomes in important ways.

Illness

Assistance during extended illness is the predominant form of helping behavior in the community.[11] The lack of on-site services, complications involved in requesting help from outside agencies,[12] and a disinclination to use community resources all contribute to the degree to which tenants rely on one another during episodes of infirmity. Sharing a common awareness of the increasing likelihood of sickness with advancing age and a fear of institutional settings, residents often help each other in ways that extend their ability to live independently.

For some, belonging to a friendship network increases the reliability and amount of available help. Reciprocity in these instances is reinforced by obligations resulting from close ties and consists of gratitude, affection, and expectations of similar returns, should the need arise. One woman in her late seventies signed herself out of the hospital against her doctor's orders after a severe heart attack because she felt she received better care from her friends in the building: "They treated me so badly in the hospital. I wasn't washed properly, and they left me sitting up too long in a wheelchair. This made me want to get back to my room all the sooner. Anytime I'm sick like this there are people here to help me. They do my shopping and cooking, and my friend Grace—who just lives down the hall—comes in every day to give me a massage. I'd be in a nursing home right now if it wasn't for all these people who are so good to me. And I've helped them often enough in the past."

A number of tenants, however, lack networks of close friends and consequently must depend on the largesse of neighbors and passersby. For this group, living in close proximity to similar others substantially increases chances of making contact, but relying on the willingness of others can be a risky affair when needs are great and friends are few. Some use highly persuasive techniques for insuring needed assistance. One woman recovering from a severe gastrointestinal attack kept her door open and blew a whistle when she needed some food from the corner store. Some expressed irritation about this abrasive method of attracting attention, but invariably, at least one person would come in to see what she wanted. Another man who was unable to speak because of a throat infection also left his door ajar and rang a small bell. Anyone pausing to see what the disturbance was about received a prepared note containing requests for food, medicines, or the daily paper. Acceptance of the slip of paper represented a form of contractual obligation from which it was difficult to withdraw.

Payment in the form of money or material goods is another effective way of securing needed assistance. Judy Simpson, aged seventy-eight, is a retired practical nurse who sometimes performs maintenance chores for a small fee, but these arrangements do not always go smoothly, as the following example illustrates. One day while we were having a cup of tea in her apartment, Judy told me how she cooked and cleaned twice a day for this man who was recovering from a heart attack. He paid her fifty dollars a month, and when she asked for more money he became abusive and swore at her. "After all I did for him, and he treated me like that! He's a mean man and nobody likes him. So I decided to quit. I tried to call his cousin and get her to come in to help. But she told me he was so mean she had given up trying to do anything for him." Within a month the ailing tenant was removed to the hospital, where he later died. In this situation the costs of providing assistance were perceived as exceeding the small monetary rewards involved, and help was terminated, with negative consequences for the aid recipient.

Another tenant who was a lay preacher tended to the daily needs of a neighbor bedridden after a severe stroke. Although professing Christian motives for helping, he described how he was paid very well for his efforts. "Mr. Myers must have given me over five hundred dollars in clothes. Some were expensive suits, and there were a couple of overcoats. Maybe they're a little out of style now, but they can still be worn. He didn't have to give me these things, but he kept urging me—so I took them." Conversations with both men indicated that friendship was not a basis for these transactions. On one occasion Mr. Myers confided to me that he considered "the old preacher a crazy old guy who would steal you blind if you were careless enough to leave any money around." Carefully over the next five months he doled out his wardrobe, and at the end of that time he died quietly in the familiar surroundings of his own room.

There are some constraints on the provision of assistance during illness. Requests for help need to be seen as legitimate in relation to existing needs. Incapacitated residents are expected to demonstrate at least some efforts at self-help within the limits of their abilities, and those who are perceived as taking advantage of their situation by making excessive demands are negatively sanctioned. An expectation of recovery is also important. The performance of services for those perceived as recuperating becomes meaningful when many share similar beliefs about the inadequacies of care in medical settings. When tenants are judged terminally ill, however, and when levels of physical deterioration become highly visible to the rest of the community, there is a decline in the impetus to help, and many become increasingly critical of supportive efforts to prolong residential status.

An example of this occurred in a situation involving a man who was in the terminal stages of Lou Gehrig's disease. He consistently ran away from medical settings to return to his own apartment (see the case history of Armen Saroyan, Chapter 7). The extent of his physical decline was readily apparent to others because he frequently left his room to spend time in the lobby. Although he expended considerable effort to look presentable, he drooled excessively and was only able to move slowly with the aid of a walker. When it became known that I was providing him with considerable assistance, several tenants were outspoken in their criticism of my efforts, as the following conversational exchange illustrates. "Why are you helping that guy in 805?" one man asked, as he saw me leaving Armen's room. "They shouldn't let him stay on here. He doesn't belong anymore. It's demoralizing to see the way he creeps around, and when you're like that, it doesn't do much good for a bunch of people to be running around doing things for you. A nursing home is where guys like that belong." In a community where all are vulnerable to the possibilities of illness and death, the noticeable presence of the terminally ill who exhibit severe levels of physical deterioration constitutes a threatening reminder of possible outcomes.

Overall, constructing and maintaining support systems during times of extended illness becomes a crucial factor in the ability to remain independent and avoid confinement in medical settings. Membership in friendship networks does increase the likelihood of receiving help, but many must depend on the willingness of others who happen to be in the vicinity. Compassion and caring are indeed influencing variables, but more often motivations for helping are influenced by notions of reciprocity in some form, which can range from monetary payments to more generalized assumptions that such acts constitute a form of investment against future needs. Thus expectations of returns are of an indeterminate, open-ended character that extends the availability of help to greater numbers when the occurrence of health losses is unpredictable.

Emergencies

Crisis situations with life-and-death consequences occur with understandable frequency in surroundings where many are over the age of seventy-five. Examples of such events are heart attacks, fainting spells, accidents involving bodily injuries, acute complications arising from long-term illnesses, and death. These situations differ from extended illness in the immediate intervention that is often required. Whether help is in time depends on the effectiveness of discovery procedures, which in turn are affected by factors of living alone, degrees of sociable involvement, and alertness by others to signs of possible trouble.

In a public housing project of this kind, the presence of a security guard and staff whose job definitions encompass a wide variety of caretaking functions affords greater degrees of protectiveness than would generally be found in commercially owned facilities. Capacities of official personnel to detect crisis situations are necessarily limited, though, by the small staff size and structural features of the building. It is an impossible task for one security guard to check on every tenant, and there are no alarm systems in the apartments. Although each tenant receives a large pink card that can be pushed under the door in case of emergency, one resident wryly observes that the card is of little use if one has already passed out on the floor. Most apartments have phones, but at night the guard is often out of his office on patrol and there is no other person around to take incoming calls. In many instances tenants thus need to rely on their own efforts in the discovery of emergency situations and the provision of needed help.

Often residents intervene directly without the aid of a staff member. Herbert Watson, a man in his late sixties with a past history of heart disease, describes how he obtained skilled assistance when he unexpectedly fainted in his room: "When I came to, I dragged myself over to the phone. I was too frightened to stand up because I didn't know if I would fall over again and maybe break a leg or a hip. No one was in the office, so I called this lady upstairs who is a practical nurse. She came right down and helped me over to the bed. She took my blood pressure and said it was way down. After a while I was O.K., but she stayed with me until she was sure I could manage."

In other situations residents act in an intermediary capacity and notify the security guard or the manager's office when medical help such as an ambulance is needed. One woman who was suffering from sudden abdominal pains managed to knock on her neighbor's door before collapsing in the outside hall. Fortunately the resident was at home, and he quickly located the security guard, who called for an ambulance. In another instance a tenant was on her way to the bingo game on the third floor when she encountered a man sitting on a couch by the elevators. Sensing that something was wrong, she asked if he needed help. When he failed to reply she quickly asked a passing tenant to find the security guard while she stayed with him to supply some comfort and support. Medical help arrived in time, and he was taken to the hospital.

Whether the situation is defined as an emergency depends on the assessment of whether the consequences will acutely affect the well-being of the afflicted person in the immediate present (Krebs 1970; Latane and Darley 1970) and on the perceived legitimacy of the need for help. Judgments that a crisis is occurring are promoted by ready observation of demonstrated symptoms such as passing out as well as by personal knowledge of the kinds of crises that can happen in an environment where all share the status of being old. People are also much more likely to intervene when they perceive the situation as resulting from factors beyond the victim's control than when they consider it a consequence of personal deficiencies (Berkowitz 1972; Schopler and Matthews 1965). For example, health crises are qualitatively different in terms of worthiness from situations involving passing out from excess alcohol consumption.[13] Tenants are far more inclined to provide assistance to the victim of a heart attack than to a known drinker who passes out in the lobby. One man who had an established reputation for drunkenness received no help from residents when he fell down in front of the elevator after an evening spent at the corner bar. He slept there until morning, when the janitor finally helped him up to his room. The greater the inclination of bystanders to redefine the situation as one not deserving direct involvement, the less will be the tendency to interpret the situation as a critical event.

These definitions are also critically affected by processes of discovery. In public areas such as the hallways, elevators, and downstairs lobby, quick detection is a simple matter. For those habitu-

ally using the back stairs to avoid the lobby crowd, possibilities
of being found decrease. On his way to take an early morning
walk, one man tripped and struck his head on one of the stairs.
He lay there unconscious and bleeding for over an hour before he
was discovered by the custodian.

For others, the chance of being found in time of crisis is increased by the existence of intimate ties with other residents. The
death of one man was quickly discovered when a friend living
on another floor came down to see why repeated phone calls remained unanswered. In another situation an elderly man who had
just returned from the hospital experienced a heart seizure in his
room. Within an hour he was found by a neighbor who visited
him daily, and needed medical help was obtained in time. In describing this event, one tenant remarked that someone was always
going in and out of this man's apartment, "but a lot of people living around here could be dead in their room for days without anyone finding them."

For a significant number, low levels of social involvement and
desire for privacy undermine possibilities of being found. Some
tenants have the reputation of rarely being seen and only emerge
periodically from their rooms to attend to necessary errands. In
their case, long absences from public view are expected and not
being seen around fails to arouse suspicions that something is
amiss. Known alcoholics are in greater danger of remaining un-
discovered than others. Public tolerance of excessive drinking
combined with the expectation that drinking binges can go on
for several days or weeks places such people in an exempt status
where customary surveillance modes are frequently inoperative.

A few residents have voluntarily become self-appointed custo-
dians for their individual floors. They maintain a vigilant eye for
indicators of trouble: mail not being collected for several days,
unanswered phones, official notices accumulating in front of
apartment doors, and failure to be seen in public areas such as the
lobby for undue lengths of time. They request that available staff
members check such situations out. Clara Barstow, who is labeled by some as a nosy busybody for her efforts, describes her
reasons for keeping watch in this way: "I don't know a lot of

people on my floor, but when I haven't seen anyone for awhile, I'll ask the janitor to go with me to their rooms and unlock the door. A couple of times we've found people dead. But anyway, I think it's important to do this—not because I like the people around here; some are real mean—but because this is something that needs to be done—that's all."

The effectiveness of these informal surveillance procedures is limited compared with the efficiency of the built-in alarm systems often used in retirement housing, but the efforts of a conscientious few combined with the awareness of others about the ominous consequences that can be involved when a neighbor is unaccountably absent from public view result in greater overall protection for many who live there. When a critical event is discovered, strong obligations to become involved are operative that transcend friendship obligations and likeability.[14] The stronger the perceptions of another's dependency on intervening efforts on their behalf, the greater the inclination to give help (Krebs, 1970). For residents, similarities in circumstances such as advanced age and living alone function to increase the awareness of this dependency effect. None can rely on the presence of a spouse or roommate. The existence of beliefs about the disinclination of other tenants to help can also be viewed as an influencing factor. Believing that others may not be motivated to intervene because of physical inabilities or personality inclinations can increase the sense of personal responsibility to become involved that people experience when they happened to be on the scene when a crisis occurs.

Providing assistance in emergencies is also directly affected by expectations of reciprocity, should similar circumstances arise involving the aid giver. Whereas immediate responses are indeed influenced by altruistic concerns, and a refusal to give aid to someone lying unconscious on an apartment floor would be unthinkable, a degree of self-interest is present nonetheless. Both greater alertness for signs of trouble and quick reactions in times of crisis among those living in close proximity help to reinforce community norms of obligation to act. Reciprocity in these situations is obviously indeterminate because of the uncertain nature of crises, nor can returns of similar value necessarily be expected directly from the aid recipient. But the act of providing help to nearby others who are in acute distress functions as an important form of credit against future needs affecting the welfare of all residents.

Modes of Secrecy and Assistance

One of the important cultural rules governing assistance exchanges is secrecy. In spite of the frequency with which helping activities actually happen, these events are rarely discussed in public. Although some tenants show little concern about the extent of public awareness of their needs, many are reluctant to talk about their participation in these transactions. An example of this occurred when I visited a tenant who recently returned from the hospital after extensive surgery.

When I asked if there was anyone helping him out, he replied in this way: "Of course not. Who in this place cares for me? Oh, maybe someone comes in once in a while, but they don't do much. I really have to do most things for myself and even manage to make my own meals." Later in the day I was talking to Mary Sanderson, a friendly woman I had come to know well. In confidential tones she informed me that she had just come back from this man's apartment. "Don't tell anyone," she said, "but I go up to his place every day to see if he needs any food, and I also take up his mail. Oh, he isn't the easiest person in the world to get along with, but when I was sick not too long ago he was very good to me and brought up my mail every day." She added that another friend of hers was also helping him prepare his meals.

The question then arises as to why helping behavior should have a low profile in this setting where public recognition of such acts is usually an expected and welcome form of social reward. One reason is that keeping such exchanges secret helps to extend the recipients' ability to remain in the setting in spite of increasing frailty. Although management evidences considerable leniency in this area, residents are keenly aware of staff's ability to exert pressures for removal. Some will even avoid informing the office about periods of hospitalization in their attempts to hide serious illnesses. Quietly turning to other tenants is viewed as a safer course. Sustaining public impressions of continuing competence thus becomes an important strategy for retaining residential status, when the degree of required assistance remains known to a limited few.

The covert nature of helping activities in which the identities of help providers are not widely known also limits possibilities of unwanted contacts with troublesome others and reduces fears of exploitation. Some want to avoid association with those who are seen as offensive. One woman told me that she didn't want it known that she was caring for a neighbor who was recuperating from a cancer operation. Her own health was precarious, and she was particular about the kind of person she helped. But the man she was presently involved with was "a gentleman who kept himself clean and had such nice manners."

Not all residents abide by norms of reciprocity in aid giving, and the demands of some can become exploitive, as is clearly evident in a conversation among several residents about "a sick old lady in room 716 who is always pestering people to do things for her." One of her neighbors described his negative reactions to her persistent requests: "This one day she asked me to go and get her a TV dinner. She didn't like the one I brought back, so I had to go and get her another one. Then she asked me to get some medicine at the drugstore and bring her back a paper. I don't mind helping someone, but she's really pushing it." Another participant in the conversation added that she knew who he was talking about; she had also helped her out several times. "But she's asked me too many times and she doesn't do anything to help herself. After all she isn't that sick—it isn't as if she is in bed all the time. One time she left all these bags of garbage outside her door expecting someone to come along and take them down to the garbage chute. The smell got so bad that I ended up carrying them down there myself. That got me mad, so I'm not going to help her anymore."

In a setting where needs are extensive, resources are limited, and helping activities could involve high personal costs, it is understandable why so many emphasize the importance of noninvolvement in the affairs of others and hide the extent of helping activities. According to Clara Barstow, for instance, who in reality provides considerable assistance to other residents, "Now, here in this place I don't tell nobody about my business or about who I help. That's how you get along here—just mind your own business, that's all."

Widely held beliefs about the disinclination of many to provide aid are publicly upheld. An example occurred one day when I was sitting with Minority Circle members in the lobby. Bob Williams, a tall man with sparse, graying hair, was describing the circumstances under which he did some shopping for a tenant confined to her bed: "This lady who lives just down the hall from me had her door open, and she was calling out for someone to come in. When I stopped to see what she wanted, she said she needed some food from the corner store. She was too sick to go herself. Then she said that several people had already gone by without stopping. Now I wouldn't do that—but what can you expect from some of the people who live around here who just don't care." These remarks prompted no comments critical of those who failed to respond. What happened seemed to fall within a shared set of expectations about the kind of behavior one could expect from other tenants. The conversation turned to baseball scores.

Such a reaction reaffirms the view that helping others can in some instances be an individual, discretionary action and not a binding obligation on all residents. Thus secrecy enables a certain degree of flexibility, which in the long run probably increases the overall willingness to provide help in ways that are not threatening to limited resources and personal inclinations.

In spite of the lack of intimate ties among community members and the popular beliefs about the disinclination of many to provide assistance, living at the St. Regis clearly provides access to needed assistance when health and personal losses occur. Being alone at a time when emergency situations and prolonged illnesses happen with increasing frequency, many residents remain quietly supportive of helpfulness norms. Although altruistic sentiments are in evidence, much involvement is based on utilitarian concerns. In addition to help received from staff members, assistance exchanges among tenants based on principles of reciprocity become important forms of social insurance against the negative effects of limited personal resources, and even those who are non-participants become beneficiaries.

The findings in this chapter also illustrate the importance of the social domain when one is assessing the functionality of peer-oriented reciprocal networks and the need to pay attention to the value systems that affect exchange patterns. When the resident population's preferences for assistance are expressed in terms of neighborly reciprocity and avoidance of community services, successful intervention strategies need to be predicated on naturally existing support systems and directed toward creating viable alternatives to formal services. Some suggestions appear in Chapter 8.

Chapter 6

Keeping Safe

The elderly tenants of the St. Regis live in a precarious environment. Residing in an area of high crime rates, significant numbers have been subjected to muggings and robberies over the years, and others have had vicarious exposure through the experiences of neighbors and friends. Mary Robbins, for example, is a quiet, small woman in her mid-seventies who is only able to move slowly with the aid of a cane. She was recently robbed early one afternoon by two young men close to a downtown shopping mall. A recently cashed social security check was in her purse, and her assailants successfully escaped with $125. During the struggle, Mary's right arm and jaw were broken. She spent several weeks in the hospital, and although the fractures healed, she never regained the full use of her arm.

Leaving the building at night also entails danger. One tenant describes how his neighbor was relieved of fifty dollars late one night in the alley directly adjacent to the building: "When you're carrying that much money, you're asking for it! I told John lots of times not to use the back alley, but he was really drunk this one night. I guess this guy must have followed him from the bar. He got beaten up badly and had this big bruise on the side of his face. By the time he came to and found the security guard, the guy who robbed him was hell and gone down the street."

Violent deaths are not uncommon. In the hotel next door the notorious "Slasher" killed one of his elderly victims during a murderous rampage involving at least a dozen slayings in the inner city. In response to this event, one woman resident said living so close to where such a horrible thing happened made her nervous going out the front door. In a more fatalistic vein, a man commented that there really wasn't too much to be afraid of; "after all, only one out of every two million people end up getting murdered, and that kind of thing can happen anywhere."

After I had been in the setting for a year and a half, Jesus the custodian was stabbed to death in the parking lot behind the building. As one woman tenant described the event, "It was a terrible thing. He went to get something out of his car around one o'clock in the morning. Two black guys jumped him and stabbed him twenty-three times, but all they got was a couple of dollars out of his wallet. There was a lot of noise and some of the old people living on that side of the building called the police. They did manage to get the guys who did it while they were running away. The next morning we could see all this dried blood and the outline in chalk where the body had been."

In the public recounting of this happening, expressions of regret were mingled with implied blame. By going out late at night to an area that was known to be unsafe, Jesus had disregarded basic rules of personal safety that were well known to other residents. One woman commented that "it is God's will when you have to go. But after all, he of all people should have known that going out like that is dangerous. We know that we should stay in at night."

As long-term residents of the central city, many tenants are knowledgeable about defensive strategies against criminal victimization, but increasing age with accompanying physical losses requires additional measures to reduce exposure to possible harm. Do the residents perceive their current living arrangements as affording a greater degree of protection than other housing available to low-income people in the area? In addition to formal security arrangements provided by the Housing Authority such as the presence of a security guard, to what degree are tenants themselves involved in informal surveillance tactics that contribute to the safety of their environment?

Research and Theory on Housing and Safety

Although the elderly are less likely to be victimized than other age groups (Cook et al. 1978; Goldsmith and Goldsmith 1976), they evidence greater fear of crime than do younger people (Braungart et al. 1979; Clemente and Kleinman 1976; Sunderland et al. 1980), and their place of residence affects the degree to which they experience these fears (U.S. Department of Justice 1979). For example, among the elderly residents of downtown hotels in Chicago, fears of being attacked were found to be significantly higher than among elderly homeowners in the suburbs (Bild and Havighurst 1976). The availability of housing that provides security guards, electronic surveillance, and locked exits for those of low income thus becomes an essential component in surviving successfully in urban locales where criminal attacks are a daily affair.

Elderly people living in planned, age-segregated housing appear to be less fearful of crime and less likely to be victimized than comparable populations in nonprotective, age-mixed surroundings (Lawton and Yaffe 1980; E. Sherman et al. 1975). Gubrium (1974), for example, hypothesizes that fear of crime is likely to be less in age-segregated housing because of the intimate ties that develop among age peers living in close proximity. In such groupings, the availability of friendship networks enables empathic communication that diminishes these apprehensions. In contrast, elderly people living under more isolated circumstances experience greater misgivings because of having to deal with these concerns on an individual basis.

Granting the psychological benefits derived from increased contacts with sympathetic reference groups, perceptions of safety in age-segregated housing are also affected by structural considerations including architectural features and security arrangements, the extent of outside threats, and the effectiveness of the informal protective strategies used by residents themselves. Thus another function of age-dense living is the possibility, prompted by shared concerns, of increased propensities for collective action in the construction and maintenance of defensive strategies. Concerns for personal safety are lessened when these strategies are effective.

These considerations can be profitably viewed in relation to Suttles's (1972) concept of the defended neighborhood. These areas (which can be limited to one apartment building or several city blocks) consist of clearly defined territories in urban locales within which occupants experience a greater sense of security from a threatening outside world. Such regions represent functional adaptations to the complex problems of social control in cities where formal measures are largely unable to guarantee sufficient protection and where large and ethnically diverse populations interact in conflictual ways. Within these sectors the complexities of decision making are reduced because clearly defined boundaries increase one's ability to differentiate between safe and unsafe areas and to distinguish between outsiders and those who belong. Residents in such neighborhoods assume much of the responsibility for their own protection and become actively involved in defending their territories against unwanted intruders.

The defended community model is particularly salient for lower economic groups in hazardous urban surroundings, and residential groupings of the elderly are no exception. Given the inadequacies of police protection and the reality of living in high-risk areas, many have little choice but to rely on their own resources. Under these circumstances living with similar others who share concerns for personal safety can result in greater efforts to participate in collective defensive measures. In contrast, mixed age groupings living in hotels or apartments would be less likely to become involved because of greater mobility, absence during the work day, and less concern about victimization because of age differences. In addition, age homogeneity also contributes to group safety by making the insider–outsider distinction more precise. In a population where most have wrinkled faces and graying hair, it is an easy matter to single out those who do not belong.

Similarly, in a study exploring the relationship between social class differences and attitudes toward housing, Rainwater (1966) concludes that because lower-class people are more likely to live in an environment where threats to personal safety are a familiar part of everyday existence, they are more likely to regard their homes primarily as places of refuge, which would substantially increase defensive tendencies.[1] In his investigation he also focuses on the importance of nonhuman as well as human sources of danger in perceptions of safety. Rodents, fires, poor plumbing, inadequate heating, and deteriorating buildings are equally threatening to those of deprived circumstances.

The defended neighborhood model and Rainwater's notion of the "home as refuge" among lower income groups are helpful in directing attention to the St. Regis residents' collective and individual strategies for coping with increasing needs for security at a time in life when defensive capabilities are weakening. In spite of the presence of security guards and locked doors, residents must often rely on their own abilities to protect themselves and their community against the outside world.

Perceptions of Safety and Security Arrangements

The building itself is clearly viewed as a safer place to live than other expensive hotels in the area. This attitude is evident in the comments of Tom Williams, a man in his late seventies who has lived and worked downtown for many years:

> As a senior citizen living in the central city, I've found that in the daytime it is occupied by many, many people. But come five o'clock a tremendous change takes place. A great percentage of the population—a large majority—leave the city and go to the suburbs, and the city becomes a different place. A different type of person then comes on the streets. They are not visible people—and it has become so that now, older people in particular do not feel safe if they are on the streets of our city after dark. But where I live is much better than many of the older hotels around which are run independent of the city. But even in spite of the security measures which are taken in here—security

guards, doors locked, front door locked—some people still don't feel secure. They lock their own doors—they won't admit anyone.

Another woman resident aged seventy-four expresses similar feelings: "Here in this building I feel safer. At the other hotel where I lived for six years, they didn't have any security guards and just anyone could get inside if they wanted to. Maybe the guards around here aren't the best, but at least the crooks out there know one is around, and this means they are less likely to come and rob us. Also, you get to know the people around here and you can tell who does and doesn't belong."

Living in the St. Regis is also seen as providing greater protection from the nonhuman sources of danger in the urban environment. In downtown Los Angeles major fires involving old apartment buildings happen with considerable frequency, and during the course of my research, three fires broke out in the hotel next door. As one resident states: "Now, this old place hardly got shook up at all in the 1971 earthquake. But take that old building next door—it should have been condemned a long time ago. The city people shouldn't let people live in a fire trap like that. Now this place we live in is a lot more safe. It's built of steel and concrete that doesn't burn easily. And because it's run by a public agency, they had to put in those fireproof doors. You don't find private places taking these kinds of precautions." Standards of maintenance are also upheld in accordance with Housing Authority regulations. Periodic housekeeping inspections, extermination procedures for termites and rodents, and regular repairs of plumbing fixtures provide surroundings that are physically safer than other low-rental accomodations in the neighborhood.[2]

Over the years, security measures have gradually improved in response to the occurrence of serious crimes. During the first two years, there were no security guards on the premises. Although emergency numbers were available and the janitor, who lived in the back of the building, could be called upon in case of emergency, residents were generally expected to fend for themselves between the hours of five in the evening and eight o'clock the next morning. It was only after several robberies happened inside the building and one elderly woman was raped in her room that a guard was hired to be on duty between six in the evening and two in the morning.

Some residents expressed anger about the Housing Authority's belated attempts to rectify past deficiencies: "Things had gotten so bad around here that I was standing talking to this lady in the lobby when this young woman came in the front door. She grabbed my friend's purse and got away with all her money and identification. It was only after this happened and that poor little old lady was raped that the Housing Authority decided to do something about it." Even with the addition of one guard, tenants were still without any protection between the hours of two and eight in the morning.

Security measures were finally improved a year later when, within a period of several weeks, the custodian was murdered and two residents were physically assaulted by an unknown person while waiting for a bus at seven o'clock in the morning. Coverage was then provided on a twenty-four hour basis, and currently, one guard is on the premises at all times.

The guard patrols all residential floors and adjacent outside areas at 1½-hour intervals. The times at which these inspections take place are purposefully varied to reduce the predictability of the guard's whereabouts. During these tours the following checking-out procedures are performed: inspecting the halls for suspicious outsiders; testing to see if apartment doors and exits are securely fastened; checking the main lounge and lobby for the presence of unauthorized individuals; touring the street directly in front of the building, and checking the back alley for trespassers without legitimate reasons for being there. At the end of his rounds the guard returns to his office on the third floor to be personally available to any residents needing assistance.

Although these procedures have substantially increased overall security, the size of the building and the number of exit points limit the guard's effectiveness. Exit doors leading to the back stairs are located on each residential floor, and in addition to the main front entrance, several back doors on the main floor can also be used for entering and leaving the premises. Guards often find these doors left open, and it is not unusual to encounter outsiders wandering around in the corridors or asleep on the back stairs. During a six-month period in 1977, security guard reports show thirty-two trespassers evicted from inside and areas close to the building (see Table 6.1). On one occasion, a long-haired man dressed in old, rumpled clothing was discovered asleep in the restroom on the third floor shortly after midnight. The intruder was quickly escorted out of the building and directed to the nearby Salvation Army, where he could find a place to sleep. Another time, two teenage youths were found on the sixth floor in the middle of the afternoon. When they were unable to give legitimate reasons for being in the building, they were ordered to leave or face the possibility of arrest for trespassing.

During the daytime, the main front door remains unlocked and outsiders can gain entrance in spite of the fact that their presence is quickly challenged by those sitting in the lobby. Around five o'clock the guard routinely locks the front door, and it remains fastened until the next morning. Each tenant has a master key and can enter and leave the building at any hour, but visitors arriving after hours can only gain entrance through the use of an intercom panel located outside the main door. Buzzers connect with individual rooms and residents must personally come down to let guests in.

Reactions to the improved security measures are mixed. Those recently moving in express satisfaction with current arrangements, but long-term residents feel that too much self-responsibility in protective measures is still expected. As one woman says, "I know that one guard can't be in all places at all times, and a lot of times you can't find him when you need him. But they expect us to look after ourselves and try to get by with spending as little money as they can. Some of the people around here are too old and feeble to do anything."

Many tenants, however, are actively involved in a variety of protective actions that supplement security measures perceived as deficient. The need for joint efforts in the defense of territorial

TABLE 6.1

VOLUME OF SECURITY GUARD ACTIVITIES

	January	February	March	April	May	June	Total
1976:[a]							
Trespassers caught	6	1	1	3	4	1	16
Doors found open	7	10	3	6	5	7	38
Police called[b]	0	0	0	1	0	0	1
Ambulance called	0	3	6	3	0	1	13
Deaths[c]	0	0	0	0	0	0	0
1977:[d]							
Trespassers caught	7	6	8	10	1	0	32
Doors found open	17	21	15	16	9	0	78
Police called[b]	1	0	5	4	0	3	13
Ambulance called	6	1	4	6	4	0	21
Deaths[c]	0	1	2	0	0	0	3

SOURCE: Housing Authority Security Guard Reports, 1976, 1977.

NOTE: Comparison of totals definitively shows that increased guard coverage in 1977 increased the protection given.

[a]Coverage at this time was weekdays from 6:00 P.M. to 2:00 A.M. and weekends from 10:00 A.M. to 2:00 A.M.

[b]Reasons for the calls were suspicion of a crime being committed, assistance in evicting unruly trespassers, arrest of a drunken tenant, sound of rifle fire in the street, or detention of a robbery suspect.

[c]Includes only deaths that occurred on the premises while a guard was on duty.

[d]Coverage at this time was weekdays from 4:00 P.M. to 8:00 A.M. and weekends around the clock. A year later, coverage was provided on a twenty-four-hour basis at all times.

boundaries is widely recognized, and careless behavior such as failing to report to staff members the presence of unknown persons in the building is negatively sanctioned. The kinds of defensive strategies and the degrees to which they are used are affected however, both by features of physical design and by the extent to which proprietorial attitudes are extended to areas inside and adjacent to the facility.

Spatial Definitions and Defensive Stategies

The concept of defensible space has been used to analyze safety and its correlates in a number of studies. Newman, for example, defines *defensible space* as "the range of mechanisms, real and symbolic barriers, strongly defined areas of influence and improved opportunities for surveillance—that combine to bring an area under the control of its residents" (1972:3). When this sense of spatial ownership exists, occupants of residential settings are stimulated to take up their own policing and feel they have a right to challenge intruders.

Features of physical design that encourage or discourage friendly interaction also have an important effect on proprietorial orientations (Rowles 1981). In a study of public housing projects in New York, Newman (1972) found that windows overlooking entry points and semipublic areas with comfortable armchairs that encourage sociable intercourse both brought more space under the watchful control of the residents. Studies of the ill-fated Pruitt-Igo Housing Project in St. Louis demonstrated, however, that isolated stairwells, unprotected corridors, and the lack of semiprivate places conducive to the development of neighborly relations all resulted in open spaces that were perceived as a type of no-man's-land. Instances of assault, robbery, and rape were frequent in these areas, and passing residents quickly retreated to the safety and seclusion of their own apartments (Rainwater 1966; Yancey 1973).

These findings help to explain variations in the degree to which areas within and adjacent to the St. Regis come under the protective surveillance of the tenants. Connecting hallways on the residential floors and the back staircase are seen as semipublic places, and watchful behavior there is limited because of the reluctance of many to linger. In the long corridors, visibility is limited by the lack of windows and the inadequate lighting; the unavailability of any seating discourages sociable exchanges. When getting off the elevators, tenants usually walk quickly to their own rooms, rarely lingering for conversation with others who happen to be in the vicinity. Women feel especially vulnerable, as the following comments by Evelyn Dixon, a socially active woman in her early seventies, illustrate: "I don't like to go in the halls at night. Sometimes when I've been sitting in the lobby until late and then go up to my room, I try to get inside my door as fast as I can. And everytime I leave my room I look both ways to see if it's O.K." Others dislike using the back stairs of the isolated location and easy accessibility to outsiders. Possible risks don't, however, deter a determined few who consistently use this back route to preserve the privacy of their daily affairs.

In contrast, the main lobby is viewed as a semipublic area for residents only, and the presence of questionable outsiders arouses immediate suspicion. This area can be defined as a *surveillance zone*, a space that occupies an intermediary position between "home" and the outside world (Rowles 1981).[3] Watchful behavior is facilitated by large bay windows looking out on the busy street outside, comfortable seating arrangements, access to the main entrance (see Figure 1.1), and the presence of residents over a twenty-four hour period. As the discussion in Chapter 2 illustrates, many important aspects of community life occur here,[4] and these in turn contribute to the degree to which residents guard a territory that is singularly theirs.[5]

During the daytime, the "lobby squad" maintains a scrutinizing stance toward those entering and leaving the building. The core members consist of four or five men and women who spend long hours sitting in customary chairs close to the front door or by a large desk next to the elevators. Young women and conservatively dressed people of both sexes having an official appearance are treated with politeness, but youthful men of black or Hispanic origins with long hair and wearing casual clothes meet with hostility and suspicion. Suspicious people are usually instructed to wait until the security guard is located to check them out, but residents will also handle the situation themselves.

One day while I was sitting in the Minority Circle, two young black men dressed in faded jeans and worn tennis shoes came in and stood looking uncertainly about the room. Around fifteen residents were sitting there, and for the moment, all conversation stopped. Martin Williamson, still vigorous at the age of eighty-nine stood up and, gesturing angrily with his cane, demanded to know who they were and what they were doing there. When one replied that he was looking for his uncle and gave a name Martin didn't recognize, he told them to leave. "You don't have any business here. You'd better get out or I'll call the guard." The young men looked at each other apprehensively, and left. The tension dissipated immediately, and Harold Willis, who was sitting next to me, said "He did O.K. for being such an old guy." The protective functions of the lobby squad are widely recognized and appreciated. As a seventy-four-year-old man says, "These people who sit in the lobby all the time—they serve as watchmen for the building. They help to keep out would-be prowlers from trying to get in—something thieves would be tempted to do if the place was deserted and there wasn't anybody sitting there."

On the whole, residents exhibit the greatest degree of protectiveness toward their own apartments.[6] Individual rooms represent private enclosures within which members can most successfully seal themselves off from external dangers and unwanted contacts. The importance of protecting their apartments is reflected in the extent to which many exercise caution in granting access to outsiders and use added security devices. In addition to the dead-bolt locks routinely supplied by the Housing Authority, many tenants have installed extra locks and door chains at their own expense. A number of tenants insert keyole plugs when leaving their apartments in spite of frequent directives from management prohibiting their use. These devices are small strips of metal that can only be removed with special keys. Their use would cause staff members to have to break open apartment doors to gain entry in an emergency. But from a tenant point of view, one woman says, "I don't want anyone—even the manager—to go into my room without my permission when I'm not there."

Visitors are usually asked to identify themselves before door chains are unfastened, and friends planning to come over are asked to phone ahead. Women are particularly careful; one says she even refuses to open her door to anyone except the security guard after eight o'clock at night. Some tenants, though, persist in leaving their doors open to improve ventilation or to attract attention when they need help. Others often criticize this behavior, claiming that those who engage in it deserve whatever happens to them.

In spite of added precautions, thefts sometimes occur. One woman was burglarized twice and lost an ancient mink stole and two diamond rings. Another tenant left her door open and her purse was stolen by a teenager who managed to slip into the building undetected. One man reported the loss of personal possessions while he was visiting a friend down the hall: "I cooked this meat loaf and left it on the counter to cool. When I got back it was gone. I looked in the oven and refrigerator thinking maybe I left it in there. Then I thought to check my drawer and found that my watch and about a hundred dollars in cash had been stolen too. I can understand them taking those things, but did they have to steal my dinner too?" In all these cases subsequent investigations by the security guard and police failed to discover the culprits.

The sidewalk directly in front of the main door serves as a buffer zone that comes under the protective surveillance of residents and some staff members. Loitering in this territory is a privilege extended to tenants only, and suspicious outsiders are quickly challenged. Three disheveled men settled down beside the front door at six one morning to finish the remains of a bottle of wine. Their privacy was short-lived. Two residents leaving for their early morning constitutional discovered them and went to get the security guard. The interlopers were sent on their way with threats of police arrest if they didn't move on.

In contrast, the alley directly behind the building is viewed as a no-man's-land; users do so at their own risk. High walls on either side limit public scrutiny, and the alley is only accessible through the parking lot and a side exit. Several large trash bins containing an assortment of empty cartons and discarded household items attract scavengers looking for useful pieces of refuse; winos seeking drinking privacy often sit on nearby steps and pass slow-moving hours in drowsy consumption. The isolated location of the alley prevents active surveillance, and community consensus is that people who use this route are to blame if victimized. There are many stories about the frequency of robberies in this area. Several women have had their purses stolen, and one man was relieved of his wallet containing thirty-five dollars and important identification papers. But for a determined few, considerations of privacy and expedience outweigh those of safety.

On the streets of the city, residents must rely on their own capacities for self-defense. A number of women routinely carry police whistles attached to neck chains or key rings; others carry noisemakers in their pockets and purses. One such device, called a "screecher," consists of a small metal tube divided into two sections, that when pressed together, emit a piercing noise that would effectively startle any potential victimizer. Some of the men carry knives or canes, and opinions differ as to which is the most effective. One man says, "When my friend was robbed he had a knife in his pocket, but he didn't have time to take it out when he was attacked. Now a cane is a different thing. You have it in your hand already and it's right there when you need it."

The carrying of guns is less common. A story that is told with some amusement describes how one resident pulled out a gun and fired at a surprised thief who tried to rob him in the alley. The assailant escaped and the bullet barely missed an elderly woman who happened to be following behind with an armload of groceries.[7] Another time, when I was visiting a tenant in his room, he took out a small pistol and informed me that he was now carrying it on a regular basis. The other night, returning home from a restaurant, he was hassled by "several young creeps" and wasn't going to take any more chances. He met my concern about the dangers involved in carrying such a weapon with laughter at my seeming naïveté and commented that in the world he came from you have to look after yourself the best way you can.

Socialization Processes and Safety Practices

Although many residents exhibit considerable skill in protecting themselves in the inner city, others are less proficient. For significant numbers, safety practices are taken for-granted because of

long experience in urban settings, but some who have led more
sheltered lives benefit from the socializing influences of interaction with other tenants, the staff, and visiting representatives of
the police department. These differences in self-defense skills are
succinctly described in the words of Jim Coburn, a man who
views himself as an expert in the art of urban survival:

> Many of the people here have been taking care of themselves
> for a lot of years and can take care of themselves now. But
> the ones who come here who don't know how to look after
> themselves—they're helped by some who have been here
> longer. Some of them learn quickly—the places where it's
> safe and not safe to go. These are the kind you see going to
> the police meetings they have here. And they listen carefully
> to what the police have to tell them. But the advice the po-
> lice gives them isn't always the best. A lot of the guys who
> live here have been brought up in the slums and think of the
> police as racketeers. Those who go to the meetings are the
> nice ones—those who haven't had much contact with the
> kind of stuff that goes on out on the streets.
>
> But some of the people here just don't learn. You can talk
> yourself blue in the face to some of these old ladies. The
> other night this old dame was going in the front door too
> slow. She was messing around trying to get her door key out
> of her purse and I was right behind her. I told her to hurry
> up but she got real mad and told me to mind my own busi-
> ness. She would open the door any way she pleased. But in
> acting like that, she makes it bad for the rest of us because
> some crook could sneak in the door behind her. People who
> are going to live here should know how to look after them-
> selves, and if they are dumb enough to act like that or do
> things like show their money or get caught in dark, lonely
> places—they're asking for it.

Periodic instructions from management and monthly crime
programs sponsored by the police department provide some
guidelines for safety. Notices are often posted on the bulletin
board in the main lobby emphasizing the dangers of using the

back alley and the need to keep exit doors locked. The manager also used the occasion of a meeting about new leasing provisions to remind those present to exercise greater care in reporting unauthorized people in the building.

Much of the working knowledge about safe conduct is also acquired informally through interaction with other tenants. The community grapevine functions as a major socializing influence in sensitizing residents to the kinds of crimes that can occur and to the importance of adhering to prescriptions for safe conduct. Stories about muggings and robberies elicit great interest, and even descriptions of crimes that happened several years ago are repeated as if they had recently occurred.

Harold Willis describes how this process takes place: "If you really counted the numbers of burglaries and muggings that happen around here, there really aren't so many. But you hear these stories a lot around here, and if you inquire further, you'll find these same stories are repeated over and over. What is more important is the attitude and sense of fear these old people have that these things might happen. They fear these uncertainties and live in a state of doubt about whether or not these kinds of things are going to happen to them."

The frequent reiteration of these stories results in what Gubrium (1974) has referred to as a "concern-magnifying effect." He suggests that older people living in age-concentrated housing are more likely to exhibit greater concern about crime because of more extensive communication and commonly held interests in the topic. This "leads to greater precaution taken by the elderly against crime, which in turn increases protectiveness" (250).[8] Another consequence of age-dense living, then, is increased communication promoting greater awareness of the adverse consequences of criminal attacks and the consequent necessity of acting to reduce personal vulnerability.

Negative sanctions levied against those who have been assaulted because of careless behavior also have important socializing effects. When I was exposed to numerous accounts of robberies and attacks in the early stages of the study, I was often struck by the apparent lack of sympathy for the victim when an impru-

dent act such as being out late at night was involved. In my own
social circles, reactions of listeners would more likely be typified
by statements of concern mingled with expressions of indigna-
tion about the frequency with which older people are subjected
to criminal attack. In the tough world of the St. Regis, these
kinds of sympathetic reactions seemed a luxury and somehow out
of place.

For example, one man who was robbed of several hundred dollars when he was returning by bus late one night after a successful
day at the track was extensively criticized for carrying so much
money in the first place. After listening to this story, one tenant
responded by saying he always carried a self-addressed envelope so
he could mail his winnings back to the St. Regis in case he made
a killing. "That way," he said, "those young niggers who follow
us old people home on the bus can't get our dough." Another
woman robbed outside a bank after cashing her social security
check was strongly rebuked for carrying so much money at one
time. In one man's opinion, "Some of these old ladies around here
go to the bank as soon as they get their social security check and
cash it all at once. Then they're dumb enough to carry their
money around with them all the time. They're headed for trouble
if they do that. I have the government send my check to the bank
and I only take out what I need at one time."

The absence of sympathetic reactions was particularly evident in the following account of a purse snatching that happened
late one night. As I entered the lobby, Mrs. Samuels, a small,
friendly woman in her mid-seventies, invited me to sit beside
her. She then told me how her purse had been stolen the night
before. "My friend and I were walking back after dinner with this
other man who couldn't walk very fast. He was telling us a funny
story, so we all stopped to listen. I was holding my purse in my
hand and was swinging it back and forth. I guess I shouldn't have
been doing that. Anyway, these two young Negroes came out of a
phone booth, grabbed my bag, and took off. I didn't have much
money in it, but they got my keys and all my ID. Something like
that happening makes you feel awful. I'm O.K. now but I hate to
think about it."

Later that same day Clara Barstow vehemently expressed her opinions about the stupidity of Mrs. Samuels's behavior to several residents sitting in the Minority Circle:

> This woman—you know, the one we call Baldy—what was she doing out at that time of night anyway? It was after nine o'clock. And swinging her purse like that—that was wrong! People really notice then, and what was she doing carrying a purse at that time of night anyway? When I go out, I carry what money I need in a little purse I pin to my underwear. And why did she have to come running all the way back here before she called the police? She should have used a pay phone. By the time the police got here, the kids who did it were long gone and the police couldn't do anything.

Implicit in these remarks are a number of rules taken for granted among residents. The victim's emotional response is considered insignificant in relation to the ways in which the victim's behavior violates important safety maxims. As my knowledge and understanding increased, I was able to piece together the major components of a safety code subdivided into safe practices for inside and outside of the building.

Inside

1. Come in the front door as quickly as possible so someone can't sneak in behind you.
2. Don't let anyone in the front door unless they can show they have good reasons for being there.
3. Report any strangers in the building to the guard, if you can find him.
4. Don't use the back doors for entering and leaving.
5. Don't open your apartment door to people you don't know.
6. Keep your apartment door closed and locked at all times.
7. Don't leave your apartment at night.

8. Don't hang around in the halls or be in the TV room if no one else is there.
9. Report any lost keys to the office, especially the one to the front door.
10. Keep away from tenants who are troublemakers.

Outside

1. Don't carry around any more money that you have to.
2. Don't go flashing around a wad of bills, especially in places like the bank, stores, or restaurants.
3. Don't go alone into places that are known to be dangerous, like the back alley or bad parts of town.
4. If you have to walk anywhere, don't stop along the way.
5. Don't blab about your winnings if you've made a killing at the track.
6. Don't go out alone at night; if you have to, get someone else to go with you.
7. If you get robbed, let the police know as quickly as possible.
8. Don't make change for anyone if they ask you.
9. If you must carry a purse or wallet, don't carry anything of value in it.
10. Get your keys out before you get to the front door.

These rules constitute a well-known system of social knowledge in the art of self-protection and are verbalized in instances where safety rules are transgressed.

Not all residents adhere to these safety practices. Having lived independently for years on a subsistence level, some are more inclined toward self-, rather than group, orientations and evidence little concern about how their actions might jeopardize the welfare of others. For example, security guards occasionally find exit doors on each floor propped open by small pieces of wood or keyholes filled with wads of paper. Although each tenant receives a master key, a few, who prefer to use the backstairs, become irritated by the added necessity of unlocking doors when they will only be gone a short time. Some persist in using the back alley in spite of the well-known dangers involved, and others remain unconcerned about reporting the presence of strangers in the building. These residents usually care little about negative public sanctions as they pursue activities congruent with their long-established habits and concerns. Yet in the long run those who don't conform to safety measures benefit from the advantages of living in a setting where substantial numbers participate in the kinds of collective and individual strategies that increase the amount of protection available to all.

For many residents, however, knowledge of and adherence to the safety directives amounts to cognitively restructuring a hazardous world and increases their ability to respond appropriately when danger occurs. The code also provides an interpretive framework within which events involving personal harm can be assessed, and the extensive public criticism that occurs when rules are broken discourages recurrence. Expressions of sympathy are dysfunctional and would only serve to weaken the importance of abiding by the safety rules. The emphasis on self-responsibility embodied in the code's provisions also becomes an important survival strategy in downtown areas where immediate help is frequently unavailable.

The necessity of observing these rules has collective significance, as one resident explains: "The trouble is that when one thief gets a good amount of money from one old person, this only encourages them to steal from the rest of us." When a purse snatching results in the loss of a master key, criminals could gain entrance through the front door. Residents are already at a disadvantage because of their visible frailty and their high-risk location. Successful robberies in which substantial amounts of money and valuables are taken only serve to attract victimizers to an area where "pickings are easy." Thus extensive disapproval of careless actions and the emphasis on individual responsibility for behaving in sensible ways both function to reduce the overall frequency of crime in ways that increase the security of all.

Overall, the findings in this chapter demonstrate that collective living in this setting increases the amount of protection available to all residents because of informal measures that protect community boundaries, communications processes that disseminate safety knowledge, and sanctioning procedures that reinforce adherence to safety norms. Many residents are already skilled in the art of self-protection from years of urban living. In spite of increasing frailty and the reality of daily exposure to possible criminal victimization, their preference is to remain because of the advantages that are involved. Living with others sharing similar concerns extends their capacity to do so.

These findings also suggest the feasibility of using the abilities of able residents who are willing to become involved when planning and implementing on-site security and safety services. Although the burden of enhancing protection should not be placed on those who are at greatest risk, programs making use of their capacities are congruent with lifestyles stressing the importance of self-help and independent functioning. Chapter 8 suggests ways in which natural defensive strategies can provide the basis for the implementation of some protective services.

Chapter 7

Staying at Home

The three case histories in this chapter concern a major feature of community life: retaining residency in the face of declining health. For those of limited means and increasing frailty, the task of remaining independent involves a complex interplay of individual coping ability, personality dispositions, and skill in using available resources. The personal stories of these three residents depict the ways in which these capacities coalesce to affect independent survival, and they dramatically illustrate how living at the St. Regis can be a viable alternative to institutionalization, one that permits some continuity with established lifestyles.

Admission to a convalescent home or hospital is usually irreversible and initiates entry into the death and dying process. Poverty, living alone, and limited family and friendship networks increase vulnerability to custodial care. Consequently, it is not uncommon for residents to run away from medical facilities before being formally released, and some will even jeopardize their well-being by refusing needed medical attention.

There is considerable variation among tenants in both level of physical decline and ability to secure needed help when crises occur. Some retain considerable vigor into advanced old age; others are less fortunate and must contend with severe losses. Many are able to construct and maintain viable support systems that extend their ability to stay on; others can pay a heavy price when self-maintenance needs exceed available help. But regardless of personal circumstances, all share similar apprehensions about the negative features of institutional care, and those caught in the downward spiral of physical decline wage a determined struggle to remain at home—often in the face of overwhelming odds. The following accounts reveal the degree of effort that this struggle can entail.

The first study describes my contacts with Armen Saroyan, a seventy-seven-year-old man who was terminally ill. In spite of the gravity of his condition, Armen was relatively successful in constructing a support system that enabled him to stay in his apartment beyond expected limits. Management and other tenants who witnessed his fight to remain independent expressed a dichotomous mixture of admiration for his tenacity and resentment of the demoralizing effects of his continued presence as the extent of his physical deterioration became more visible.

The next case depicts the struggle of a woman who was less fortunate. Over a six-month period I witnessed Miriam Davis's attempts to avoid hospitalization in the face of increasing blindness and limited ability to care for herself. Her fear and dislike of medical settings were typical of other tenants, and she continually ran away from hospitals and nursing homes in spite of the objections of health professionals. She eventually lost her room in the earlier stages of her illness and became more vulnerable to the possibilities of institutional placement.

In contrast, the last study portrays a woman highly skilled in securing needed assistance after a series of severe heart attacks. Sara Ross was a well-known figure in the community, and although she had a reputation for drunkenness and spreading malicious gossip, four or five other tenants regarded her as a close friend and provided devoted care. She in her turn had frequently provided aid to other residents in the form of household assistance and basic nursing care, sometimes for small payments, other times simply for friendship. But in the months of our acquaintance she was more often the recipient of aid because of rapidly declining health.

Armen Saroyan, Aged 77

Armen was born around the turn of the century in Turkey, of Armenian parentage, and he experienced the loss of many family members in the massacre of 1915. For several years he was forced to serve in the Turkish army, and while still a young man, he emigrated to the United States. Initially he settled in New York City, where he married and pursued the upholstering trade. Tiring of the cold winters and seeking a better way of life, he and his wife moved in 1939 to California, where their marriage eventually ended in divorce. There were no children by this union, although his wife had one son by a former marriage. Before retiring at the age of seventy, Armen had worked as an upholsterer in the film industry for twenty years.

When I first met Armen he had been living at the St. Regis for four years and was then totally dependent on social security benefits and SSI for financial support. He had the reputation of being a heavy drinker and a dedicated follower of the horses. Few seemed to like him and many were critical of his quick temper and penchant for caustic comments. A year before I knew him, he had been informed that he had Lou Gehrig's disease (a terminal illness involving slow deterioration of the nervous and musculatory systems), and his physical condition had rapidly deteriorated. Although he was still ambulatory when I met him, walking was a difficult task, and he had lost the use of his vocal cords. In spite of increased needs for supportive care, he resisted hospitalization and preferred to rely on his own remedies: patent medicines and an assortment of vitamins.

At this point in his life there were no family members or close friends that he could rely on for assistance. He was not in contact with his ex-wife and was estranged from his stepson, who refused to have anything to do with him. Occasionally he had visited with a cousin living in the area, but their last meeting had ended in angry words. Housing Authority efforts to enlist the help of these relatives when he became seriously ill met with little success. Both claimed he was impossible to deal with and wanted nothing more to do with him.

After I had been in the building for several weeks, the receptionist suggested Armen might appreciate a visit from me. She was fully acquainted with the details of his physical condition and thought there might be something I could do for him. "I don't know how he makes it," she added. "Other people with his kinds of problems would be dead by now."

It took a long time for Armen to answer the door. I saw a small man with thin, gray hair and a deeply lined face, in a soiled T-shirt, a pair of worn-out pants, and no shoes. He communicated with me by writing on a small pad he kept on a nearby table.

When I had introduced myself and explained my helping functions, I asked if I might come in and visit for a while. He agreed and proceeded to write a note describing his dissatisfaction with his present doctor. As far as he was concerned, all doctors were "no good." The prescribed medication was doing nothing for him and only made him sick to his stomach. He felt it was better to rely on his own supply of drugs and indicated a small side table covered with an assortment of patent medicines such as pain relievers, vitamins, Geritol, Bromo-seltzer, and Ex-lax. When I asked if I could provide any help with his grocery shopping, he wrote down that he was still able to go to the store and felt the exercise did him good. He could also do his own cooking, he wrote, and pointed to a small pot on the stove containing a bubbling mixture of rice and oatmeal. Having lost the ability to chew, he could now only eat soft foods, but he felt his diet was adequate and showed me his supply of milk, eggs, and yogurt in a small refrigerator. I got the impression he was somewhat suspicious of the reasons for my presence and may have thought I was sent by the office to evaluate his continuing capacity for self-care, but eventually he shared with me some details of his personal history, and as I got up to leave, he indicated he would like me to come again. With a sad expression on his face he wrote, "Sometimes I think it too difficult to go on. I'm gonna buy hole in ground."

Several weeks later, as I was entering the lobby, I caught sight of Armen sitting in a chair by the mailboxes, waiting for the mailman. At first it was difficult for me to recognize him because of his altered appearance. Here, in public view, he was dressed in a well-tailored, brown sports jacket, a bright yellow shirt, neatly pressed gray slacks, and a soft felt hat adorned with a feather. Knowing how difficult it was for him to move around, I found myself thinking of the effort and time that must have been involved in achieving this transformation. But here he was, looking remarkably alert in spite of the seriousness of his condition, nodding to other residents as they passed by. He smiled broadly upon seeing me and we planned my next visit to him in a few days.

At the appointed time I arrived at his apartment. The door was open and when I entered, he quickly wrote out: "I want you call Dr. Clark [his present physician]. My tongue getting very fat—hard to breath. I can't swallow food. I want to go to hospital." Quickly I went down to my office and called his doctor, who made arrangements for an ambulance to pick him up within the hour.

When I returned, Armen indicated that he wanted my assistance in packing his suitcase. Following his instructions I took down a plastic overnight bag on the top shelf of his closet and placed in it his ragged, terry cloth bathrobe. Slowly he moved over to the bureau, and as I opened each drawer he pointed to the items he wanted to take: a new pair of shorts, two freshly washed T-shirts, several pairs of socks, and a pair of slippers. He then went into the bathroom and brought back his shaving brush and razor. A bottle of vitamin C and some aspirin were the last articles to be included.

Now all seemed to be in readiness and we sat down to wait for the ambulance. He seemed sad sitting there in his chair and I found myself speaking encouragingly about his decision to go to the hospital. Perhaps there they would be able to make him feel more comfortable. In response he wrote down: "I don't know if I come back. Come and see me. Also make them [the attendants] take me to Lincoln Hospital. If they wont, I wont go." Then from his wallet he withdrew his Medicare card and placed it, ready, on the table. He seemed to know what needed to be done.

In about half an hour there was a knock on the door and two young men entered, pushing a stretcher. In loud voices they began telling Armen how to lie down on the conveyance. I interrupted, saying that although he was unable to speak his hearing was not impaired. Armen then indicated that he wanted to take his walker with him, but one of the men explained he would be able to obtain one at the hospital. Armen shook his head and again pointed to his walker. Jokingly the man said he could take it with him but there would be a slight charge of seventy-five dollars. When Armen shook his head, puzzled, the attendant admitted he was only kidding.

Once assured he could take his walker and that he would be going to the hospital of his choice, Armen slowly rose from his chair and looked around his small room. Becoming impatient with the amount of time he was taking, one of the men helped him onto the stretcher and, with a few deft movements, strapped Armen securely in place. I placed his overnight bag beside him and he held tightly onto my hand. We proceeded to the elevator and through the main lobby to the waiting ambulance parked by the front entrance. Around a dozen people were in the lobby, and as we passed the conversation became somewhat subdued. Some rain was beginning to fall, and one of the attendants tucked an extra blanket around Armen as they settled him in the back of the vehicle.

Reentering the lobby, I went over to the Minority Circle to see how some residents were reacting to what had just taken place. Matter-of-factly, Charles Mason commented that Armen would probably be back by tonight if the hospital felt nothing could be done. "That's what they do with people like him," he added pessimistically. Conversation then resumed with comments about yesterday's horse racing results. I seemed to be the only one who was emotionally upset.

Several days later I visited Armen in the hospital and brought him a pint of yogurt, one of his favorite foods. Quickly he grasped my hand and wrote down how glad he was to see me. He was scheduled for surgery the next morning to alleviate his difficulty in swallowing. He was afraid of what was going to happen and wanted to go home. He wrote down that every day he stayed in the hospital he got weaker. At least back at the St. Regis he was able to exercise every day, but here, all he did was lie in bed. "Back home I make kind of food I can eat. Here food is hard for me to swallow," he wrote. Then he added that at least a half dozen doctors had been in to see him and he had heard them saying that he was a hopeless case. I tried to reassure him about the impending surgery but as I left, tears came to his eyes.

Later in the same day I was talking to the manager and mentioned my visit with Armen. She expressed sympathy about his condition and said she was surprised he had stayed in the hospital so long. He had been hospitalized several times in the past, and it was his pattern to run away at the earliest opportunity. For instance, when he had a broken hip several years ago, he had somehow managed to sign himself out and return to his apartment in a taxi. "And once people like him are back here, there is no way we can make them go back unless they are declared mentally incompetent," she added.

A week after this conversation, the receptionist informed me that Armen had returned by cab the day before. I exclaimed that this was impossible because of his recent operation. When I had last seen him I had felt he would probably never leave the hospital alive. The receptionist smiled and said this wasn't the first time this had happened. "I guess he's got a right to live," she added quietly.

I went directly to Armen's apartment and found him sitting in his usual chair, reading his mail. When he saw me he smiled and gestured for me to come in. I was shaken by his physical appearance. His face was pale, and there was a fresh incision across his throat about four inches long. The stitches were still in place and the wound appeared clean and uninfected. I found myself saying, in shocked tones, "My God, what are you doing home from the hospital? How can you possibly manage?" Taking his pad he responded, "I signed myself out because I cant eat what they got. The black nurses laugh at way I eat and they want to get rid of me. My throat is worse. The operation was no good. Those doctors no good."

Getting down to more important business, he enlisted my aid in taking care of some banking details and answering several letters related to his recent medical bills. Further, he wanted me to purchase a money order so he could pay his rent and also to buy him some groceries. For the next two hours I was busily occupied in filling these requests. When all had been completed and I had delivered the groceries to his apartment, he wrote down, "Thank you. I gave you much trouble today." As I was leaving I asked if I could call his doctor to arrange for a follow-up appointment; his response: "Dont hurry." Later that afternoon I spoke with the custodian, who told me that Armen had asked him to clean his apartment every week for ten dollars.

I continued to see Armen at least twice a week and provided what assistance I could. I deposited his pension checks in the bank and made telephone inquiries about some medical bills he had received. At the corner store I purchased yogurt, eggs, and other soft foods for him to eat. Although his stitches were now removed and his doctor felt the operation was successful, Armen's physical condition did not improve, and he now only left his room on rare occasions. Then, after several weeks, he collapsed in front of a neighbor's door and once again was taken to the hospital.

When I visited him there I expected to find him close to death, but I found him sitting up in bed, reading a magazine. Again he expressed frustration about the treatment he was receiving: "I am laying here for nothing. No medications. No treatment. Waiting for day I die. Why should I live and suffer? This surgery on my throat made it worse than before. Those doctors dont know about my condition. They dont care about me." He was fearful about eventual confinement in a nursing home and added, "A convalescent home is waiting to die. I want to keep out as long as I can."

Armen gave me a carefully worded note prepared in anticipation of my visit. In it he instructed me to send a Medi-Cal sticker to the ambulance service and to order a new pair of glasses from his optometrist. His bifocals were no longer adequate and he was having headaches. On my way out, a nurse told me she felt Armen could no longer function outside of a medical setting and that I should help him plan for admission to a nursing home.

It was beginning to sound like a repeating record. Three days after I had seen him at the hospital, the receptionist told me, once again, that Armen was back in his room. "It's incredible how he's able to keep coming back when he's so sick," she re-marked. "I really have to admire him for his determination—but you know he shouldn't really be here now, because I doubt if he can even feed himself."

When I went to his room Armen wasn't there. Instead I dis-covered him sitting in his usual chair in the lobby, dressed in his good sports jacket, matching slacks, and favorite hat. When he saw me he indicated he wanted me to go with him upstairs and slowly rose from his chair. I moved to help him, but here in front of others he waved me away with an impatient gesture. Leaning heavily on his walker, he moved carefully toward the elevator and I walked beside him.

Once in his apartment he had the usual number of errands for me to perform, which included replenishing his supply of patent medicines, making a bank deposit, and writing several letters. Carefully he wrote down the brand names of vitamins and diges-tive aids he wanted me to buy and directed me to go to a nearby drugstore where senior citizens received a discount. He was still of the opinion that his doctors were incompetent and he was more successful doctoring himself. I attempted to help him face the reality of his deteriorating health and his need for special-ized care, but he ignored my remarks and restated his belief that somewhere there was a cure, if only his condition could be properly diagnosed. And purposefully changing the subject, he wrote down some details he felt should be included in a letter he wanted me to write. He was obviously pleased to be back in fa-miliar surroundings.

A week later, while I was visiting him in his room, Armen talked about his dissatisfaction with the way the custodian was cleaning his apartment. Taking me over to the stove, he in-dicated how dirty the oven was and showed me a pile of dirty laundry that was accumulating in his closet. He was receiving a housekeeping allowance from the Department of Public Social Services and wondered if I could help him find someone who would be better. I knew of a woman who occasionally cleaned for other tenants and said I would ask her to come and see him. He also wondered if his eyeglasses were ready and instructed me to pick them up if they were. After these practical matters were attended to, he wrote, "I want to die here. I stay here until I die. I'm a hopeless case. When I come here I pick up strength. When I lay in hospital I wait for death. I hear how they handle you in rest home. Help me to live here. Get me a good housekeeper." I promised I would do all I could and again brought up the subject of his need for specialized care. But he just shook his head and resumed reading his mail as I got up to leave.

During the next month I continued to see Armen several times a week and provided what help I could. He continued to cling to the belief that his doctors were mistaken and refused to seek further medical help in spite of my suggestions. His general condition was deteriorating, and the staff became increasingly concerned about his ability to look after himself and about the demoralizing effect of his continued presence on other residents. But in the face of his determination to stay, there was little that could be done.

One day when I visited, he was sitting in his chair, dressed in his best clothes as if for a special occasion. He wrote that he was now unable to eat or drink and wanted to go to the county hospital. He also wanted me to deposit some money for him and added that if he didn't come back, he wanted this money to be spent on his funeral.

I called for an ambulance, and again we packed the few items he wanted to take. The attendants arrived without a stretcher and, instead, physically supported Armen while we all went down in the elevator. Once in the lobby, they brought a stretcher in from outside and, in full view of the lobby crowd, strapped Armen securely in place. During this process his hat slipped and covered part of his face. Meaning to be helpful I reached over and tried to adjust it, but Armen pushed my hand away and placed his hat fully over his face as he was wheeled through the lobby. One resident wondered who it was this time, and another who recognized him said it was about time he went to the hospital. Tears were in Armen's eyes as he was lifted into the back of the waiting vehicle. I was crying, too, and told him I would come to visit him in the hospital, but I don't think he was paying much attention to what I was saying. Perhaps this time he knew he wouldn't be coming back.

Armen spent several weeks in the county hospital, where his general condition seemed to improve slightly because of the regular care he was receiving. I visited him several times and, upon his request, managed to secure the assistance of an Armenian priest, who provided help in making arrangements for his funeral. From his small savings account, Armen withdrew enough to pay for a casket and burial plot. He now seemed to have accepted the reality of his impending death and expressed a need to put his affairs in order. Through a set of fortunate circumstances, the priest was also able to locate Armen's long-lost brother, who was still living in Turkey; and before Armen's death, they exchanged several letters. Armen's brother expressed his continuing affection and concern.

Armen was moved to a convalescent home, where he died a month later. On the day of his death I happened to visit and found him comatose. I held his hand for a while and soon left, after arranging a bunch of flowers from my garden in a vase beside his bed. Several hours later the nursing supervisor called to say he had died peacefully.

Miriam Davis, Aged 77

When I first met Miriam she had been living at the St. Regis for two years. She was a short, stout woman with a round, pleasant face that was unusually free of wrinkles. Her thinning gray hair was cut short and held in place with a single barrette. She had remained in good health until several years ago, when she developed cataracts in both eyes, high blood pressure, and a digestive disorder. Periodically she attended a nearby medical clinic, but she had little faith in doctors. At one point she underwent a cataract operation for one eye, but the results were less than successful and her eyesight did not noticeably improve. Although she wore thick prescription lenses, most objects were fuzzy and she could only identify people within a foot or two of her face. Even the simple act of reading or writing a letter had become a laborious task, and a white cane was her support and partial guide in a cloudy world.

She rarely spoke of her childhood except to mention that she was an only child and had grown up somewhere in central California. She had been married and divorced twice over the years and had been living by herself since the age of forty. There were no children and she had not been in contact with any family members for many years. At times she made vague references to cousins living in the Middle West but said there had been no visiting or correspondence for at least twenty years. She often characterized herself as a loner, and although there were several women who had befriended her in the past, they had either died or moved away. At this point there was no one of special significance in her social circle, and her recreational activities consisted of shopping by herself, occasional social visiting in the lobby, riding on the bus, and attending a nearby nutrition program.

I had spoken casually to Miriam on a number of occasions in the lobby, and one day she came into my office to request assistance in locating an overdue social security check. After several phone calls and a promise from the local social security office that a search would be made, she invited me up to her apartment for a cup of coffee.

Her room was in disarray. A number of cartons were haphazardly stacked against the walls and appeared to be overflowing with an accumulation of personal items gathered over the years. She told me she hadn't passed the last housekeeping inspection and had been instructed by management to get rid of some of her belongings because of the danger of fire. "I'll go at it slowly but it's going to take me a long time," she said. As if she were beginning this task, she picked up an old shoe box and began examining the contents. Extracting some oversized hair pins, she remarked that they didn't make them like that anymore. Then she removed a rusty spring that had once been used to hold an ironing board cover in place. This item was followed by a small world globe about three inches in diameter, and this she insisted on presenting to me when she found out that I had children. Next she removed a yellowed booklet containing instructions about what to do in case of poisoning. "I guess I don't have much use for that." I thought to myself this would probably be the *only* thing she would throw away.

Agreeing with a comment I made about the difficulty of discarding meaningful items, Miriam reached into another pile and removed an old, rusted fishing rod, the one thing she claimed to be determined to keep, and proceeded to tell me about fly fishing with her second husband in the Sierras. "Often I'd be the only one to catch a fish." By this time we had finished our coffee, and I left her a short time later, still standing in the middle of the room, looking at the boxes that contained much of her former life.

In two weeks I visited Miriam again. She happily told me that her check had arrived; she was now able to pay her rent and buy some needed clothes. As we sat down to visit, I told her about my research interests, and in response she talked about her personal life. She didn't have much to do with other residents and usually kept to herself, she said, but the last time she was ill, a man she didn't know very well who lived several doors away looked in on her every day to see if there was anything she needed from the store. "When I'm sick like that, I just leave my door open and usually someone will stop by if I call out to them."

In spite of her limited eyesight, she still retained some mobility because she could usually depend on people passing by to help her cross intersections or get on the right bus. Initially she resisted going to the Hot Meals Program because she felt services like that were only for the poor. "Maybe I only get three hundred dollars a month, but I'm not like a lot of other people in this place who have been bums and drunks for years. I'm middle class and I've always supported myself. But I did go over there once to get a meal and found it was good. Besides, a lot of people like myself were there, and now I go several times a week. Sometimes I even stay for the film they have afterwards."

She used to go regularly to a market about a mile away because the prices were cheaper, but several months ago, when she was sitting on a bench waiting for the bus, a young man came up to her and asked if she had anything between her legs. "I was so scared after that and I never went back to that bus stop again. Now I do most of my shopping at the corner market. Maybe the prices are higher, but at least I feel safer."

One day I noticed Miriam sitting with another woman resident in the women's corner. When I joined them she informed me that a man had just been taken out on a stretcher. She didn't know if he was dead or alive, but someone told her his face was covered with a sheet. "You know, for lots of us who live here, there's nowhere else to go and we come here to die. And people come and go a lot here. Sometimes two or three people a week get taken out on a stretcher. Some die—some go to the hospital and get better and come back. You just never know." Our talk was interrupted by the arrival of the mailman, and Miriam left to check her mailbox. In spite of her limited eyesight, she was able to maneuver quite well between the coffee table and several armchairs. Another resident who happened to be standing there helped her to insert her key into the right slot, and she retrieved a circular addressed to "Occupant."

Two months later Miriam became seriously ill with the flu, and a neighbor called for an ambulance. She was taken to the county hospital, and although I called there several times, I was unable to find out where she was. For several weeks no one knew of her whereabouts. But one day she arrived back at the St. Regis in a taxi, wearing only a robe and slippers. When I went up to her apartment to find out what had happened, she told me in detail about her experiences.

After five or six days in the hospital she was transferred to a convalescent home. No one bothered to tell her what was happening, and she found herself seated with three or four other elderly patients in the back of some kind of station wagon. They were all taken to a nursing home somewhere in the south of the city. She was kept there for two weeks without being able to make any outside contacts. "I kept telling them I didn't want to stay there and that I wanted to come back to my room. But they treated me like I wasn't there and nobody would do anything. I didn't even have any money to make a phone call. But I finally got away. I waited until everybody had gone to some kind of meeting and just went out a side door in my dressing gown. Somebody in the street helped me get a cab and I came right back here. The man who drove me had to wait while I went up to my room to get some money so I could pay the fare." Later that same day two men in white coats apparently came looking for her, but she refused to answer the door.

Miriam was outraged by this experience and I shared her resentment. "I've always paid my own way and I don't like being treated like a down-and-outer—you know, like one of those welfare people. That county hospital and that nursing home—those places are full of people like that. But I'm not that way. So what right did they have to treat me like that?"

We began to discuss what arrangements could be made for assistance during her period of recovery. She was still very weak and found it difficult even to walk around. She felt she could manage on her own if only someone would come in once a day to help keep her place in order. Together we made plans to apply for housekeeping assistance, and in the meantime Miriam felt she could ask Jesus, the custodian, to give her a hand. "He's all right and I have a little money put by to pay him with." I also tried to urge her to make another appointment with her own doctor at a nearby clinic for follow-up care, but she resisted, saying that at this point, she had more faith in her own remedies.

A few weeks later, while I was visiting in her apartment, Miriam complained that she wasn't feeling well. Her face was drawn and she was experiencing frequent digestive upsets. With her permission, I arranged for an appointment at a clinic, and she promised to go the following week. I then made some soup and cleaned up the few dishes in the sink. Jesus was now coming in every day, and one of her neighbors was helping buy groceries. At least for the time being she was able to manage on her own.

She then asked me to help her decipher some mail because she was only able to read printed materials with a magnifying glass. The next half hour we spent going over accumulated mail, and in the pile was a letter containing an application for Homemaker Chore Service. I helped Miriam fill out the form and promised to mail it that same day. It was hot and muggy and we were both perspiring in the close air of the apartment. I left quietly, as Miriam lay back on her bed and closed her eyes.

Several months passed and Miriam's health improved somewhat. On one occasion when I was in her room she expressed more concern about getting rid of some of her possessions. The office had sent her another reminder, and she was upset at her inability to decide what to throw away. "Places I've lived in before were a lot bigger and there were more closets to store things in." She then confided that she was certain someone was coming into her room while she was sleeping to steal her things. She usually wore the key to her apartment around her neck on a chain, but yesterday, as she was tidying up, she looked down and the key was gone. "Now somebody must have come in here and stolen it when I wasn't looking. There are lots of people out there who have a key to my room and they can just come in any time and take my things. So far I'm missing a gold chain and my Timex watch. I've looked and looked and can't find them anywhere." Together we talked about the need to hide her more valuable possessions carefully and to obtain another key from the office.

Two weeks later Miriam happily showed me how nicely Jesus had rearranged her possessions. "He stacked everything so neatly and we only had to get rid of a few things," and indeed the small living area did present a more orderly appearance. Smaller cartons were placed in several large boxes that were arranged less conspicuously against the far wall. Having passed the housekeeping inspection, she was filled with relief that this problem was finally taken care of.

She went on to describe how it was becoming harder now to do things for herself. Even the simple task of making her bed took a long time and required considerable effort. She could still make her own meals but her food preparation was reduced to ready-made meals. Now her diet consisted primarily of TV dinners, canned goods, milk, and fruit. When I asked if she had kept her appointment at the clinic, she said she had, but she felt there was little they could do for her. Her eyes were chronically bad, and they only gave her more stomach medicine and some blood pressure pills. She was still hopeful, though, that her condition would improve. "For old people like us," she concluded, "they figure they can't do much anyway."

After I returned from a month's vacation, one of Miriam's neighbors informed me that she had once again been taken to the hospital. "This happened a while ago," he said. "I was looking in on her every day, but she got so sick that I got the security guard to call an ambulance for her. I don't know where they took her." From the ambulance service I was able to obtain the name of the hospital where she was admitted, and after several calls, I discovered that she had again been transferred to a nursing home.

I called and made arrangements to visit her in several days. I found the facility clean, well appointed, and surrounded by an attractive garden. Miriam was sitting on the edge of her bed fully clothed, and when I entered her room, she expressed pleasure and relief that I was able to find her. She said this place was better than the last one she was in, but her suitcase containing all her clothes and a portable radio was missing. The loss occurred somewhere during the hospital admission process, and now all she had to wear were two dresses and a nightgown supplied by the nursing home staff. I promised to see if I could find out where her belongings were, but she expressed skepticism about my ability to do anything about it: "They steal everything in these kinds of places."

"Do I still have my room? I tried to call there but I couldn't make the phone work—it kept returning my money. Maybe I don't have my place any longer." I was uncertain about what to tell her because I was not familiar with Housing Authority policies when residents were gone for long periods, but I assured her I would try to find out and let her know as soon as possible. Miriam felt that if she couldn't go back she would be able to find a room elsewhere—some place where the rents wouldn't be too high.

In discussing her physical condition she told me that she had only seen a doctor once since being there and he had told her very little. "I guess they want to keep me here for a while, and I know I'm too sick to leave right now anyway." I could see that she was very weak. While we were talking, she moved from the bed to a nearby chair and in the process almost lost her balance. As I moved to help her, she held tightly onto my hands to steady herself. Soon it was time for me to leave, and I reiterated my promise to find out about her missing suitcase and about her room.

When I returned to the St. Regis a few hours later, I stopped in the lobby to tell Charles Mason about my visit with Miriam. He had befriended her on several occasions in the past and said he was glad to hear she was in a nursing home, where she could be properly looked after. Later in the day, the manager informed me that because of the length of time Miriam had been gone and her poor state of health, it was no longer possible to hold her room. "I'm sorry for her," the manager added, "but even while she was living here, she could hardly get around. So we cleaned out her room—but we'll keep her things until she can make other arrangements." She had already called the nursing home and someone was coming over to pick up Miriam's clothes. The manager took me into the storage room next to her office and showed me several cartons filled with Miriam's things. In one of the boxes I could see several pans, a stained coffee pot, a few pairs of worn shoes, and a heating pad. Over in the corner was her fishing rod. "I wonder why she still has that?" the manager remarked.

A few days later, just as I entered Miriam's room at the nursing home, the recreation director came by to let me know that she had picked up some of her clothes and would shortly be bringing them up to her room. "But I couldn't bring all your other stuff back because we're short of space here," she added. Miriam reacted quickly and angrily: "You mean I don't have my room anymore?" "That's what they told me," the director replied. "But believe me, we want to see you get out of here as fast as possible, just as soon as you're well enough. And if it will make you feel any better, I'll give you an itemized list of all the things I was able to bring back."

"Yes, you better do that," Miriam retorted. As the director left, Miriam turned to me for confirmation. At least I was able to tell her that the manager had promised to store her things for several months, but I also had to tell her that I had been unable to trace the missing suitcase. Quietly Miriam asked if her fishing pole was still among her things. Then she wondered if the custodian might like to buy it. "I don't think I'll be needing it any more," she added softly.

I tried to talk about possible alternative living arrangements such as a board-and-care facility where she could receive some assistance in looking after herself. But Miriam rejected this idea and went on about her anger at being kept in this nursing home against her wishes: "What right do they have to keep me here? I know I could do all right on my own now. All I want is my own room where I can eat the things I want and do what I want. Here everything is done for you. I can't have my own money—I don't even have any rights over my own time. I tried to go out the front door the other day just to take a short walk, but someone came and pulled me back inside. So it's almost like I'm in prison, and this is a violation of my rights. I haven't done anything wrong. Why can't I come and go as I please?"

I tried convincing her of the realities of her limited eyesight and her need for medical help at this point, but to no effect: "Why I've been getting along just fine with my bad eyesight for a couple of years. People around me at the St. Regis and out on the streets usually helped me out." When she got out of this place she thought she would be able to find a room in some hotel. At least she knew her money was all right because she was having her social security checks deposited at her bank. "I don't need anyone to help me, and I'm not going to stay in this place much longer."

On the way out I stopped to discuss Miriam's situation with the recreation director, who was standing by one of the nurses' stations. She showed me Miriam's chart, on which was written the diagnosis "chronic brain syndrome and chronic hypertension," said Miram's condition was really serious and she should be there for at least a while longer. I explained at some length Miriam's need to find other accommodations soon where she could experience more freedom in her activities. The director knew of several good board-and-care facilities and said she would make a referral as soon as possible. I was frustrated and upset during this exchange by my inability to provide more decisive help. Miriam's needs for independence had come up against the reality of her declining health, and it was difficult to see what could be done.

Several weeks later the nursing home called to tell me that Miriam had consented to be transferred to a board-and-care facility. When I called her there, Miriam promptly informed me she was dissatisfied with the place. The food was always cold, and she didn't like the old lady she had to share a room with. She was determined to find another place soon. We made plans for me to visit her in several days, but when I called to confirm our arrangement, the woman in charge told me that Miriam had disappeared. That was the last time I heard anything about her. Phone calls to medical facilities and hotels in the downtown area revealed nothing, and her eventual fate has remained a mystery.

Sara Ross, Aged 76

I first came in contact with Sara after I had been at the St. Regis for six months. She was a woman of medium height with an angular face dominated by large, bright-blue eyes. During periods of sobriety she would dress in the latest fashion, but when drinking heavily, she was more apt to wear old-fashioned housedresses that did little to complement her appearance. In her mid-twenties she had married a man considerably older than herself, and together they lived happily in a small town in southern California. He died when she was in her forties, and shortly afterward she relocated in Los Angeles, where she worked as a practical nurse in a large hospital near the downtown area. She never remarried, and although she said there were some tempting offers along the way, she felt no one could take her former husband's place. For many years she lived in a residential hotel close to the hospital where she worked. After her retirement at the age of sixty-five, she continued to live there until the building was torn down to make room for a large shopping center. At this point she decided to move into the St. Regis, which had just been reconverted into a public housing project for older adults. Inexpensive rent and easy accessibility to needed services were her main reasons for moving in. Poor health and limited financial resources necessitated selling her car, so she thought it important to be within walking distance of stores, banks, and restaurants.

Sara was a sociable, outgoing person and had numerous friends in the Los Angeles area. Her family ties appeared to be nonexistent. She had been unable to have children and never spoke of any relatives. Before several serious heart attacks, Sara had been an active participant in community activities, attending bingo games and serving for several years as an officer in the Senior Citizens Club. Angered by accusations of stealing leveled against her when she was treasurer, she subsequently resigned.

Among the tenants Sara had the reputation of being a drunk, and many accused her of spreading malicious gossip. In truth, she was a heavy drinker and it was not unusual to see her weaving unsteadily through the lobby, talking incoherently to anyone passing by. But she also had a number of devoted friends in the building who defended her behavior and regarded her as a kind and thoughtful person. She was particularly close to one man who lived on the same floor. It was their habit to spend quiet evenings together watching television, and on several occasions they went to Las Vegas to try their luck at the gaming tables. Sara often stated that she didn't care if other residents thought they were having an affair. Bill was one of her dearest friends and she was appreciative of his continuing attentiveness now that so few years were left.

One day while I was knocking on the door of a nearby apartment, Sara came out of her room to tell me the occupant had been taken to the hospital. On several prior occasions we had exchanged a few words, and this time she invited me in for some homemade soup—an invitation I couldn't refuse. I was impressed by the warm, homelike appearance of her small apartment. The floor in the living room area was covered with an attractive Indian rug; on the daybed were several colorful cushions that she proudly pointed to as her own handiwork. My compliments on the attractiveness of the room pleased her, and together we sat down to bowls of delicious vegetable soup.

In response to a description of my research interests, Sara talked at some length about her own experiences in the building. She was contemptuous of the Senior Citizens Club and felt that anyone who accepted a position of responsibility in this organization received nothing but criticism in return for his or her efforts. Sara was also concerned about the declining quality of incoming residents; in her view, many of the good people had either died or moved away. "Things aren't the way they used to be," she said; yet she was satisfied with her apartment and didn't want to move because of the cheap rent and her friends in the building. An hour quickly passed and it was necessary for me to leave. She put her arms around me in a goodbye gesture and I promised to return soon.

A few days later I ran into Sara in the lobby, and she paused to tell me that a tenant she used to take care of had been taken to the hospital—"That poor man couldn't make it any longer. I'll find out where he went and send him a card," she said, before hurrying out the front door to catch a bus that had just pulled up. On another occasion when I entered the elevator, there was Sara, holding onto the wall for support, very drunk, but in a friendly mood. When we got off she held tightly to my arm and led me over to the women's corner, where she proceeded to tell me about one of her neighbors who insisted on keeping his television turned on late at night: "He's so deaf that he turns it up full blast and I can't sleep. I'd complain to that woman in the office but they never do anything." A short time later, as I started to go upstairs, Adam Johnson, a quiet, austere man who had often expressed to me his contempt for some of the residents, took me aside and confided that he couldn't stand that drunk I was talking to. "People like that shouldn't be allowed to stay here," he added, as he went off to pick up his mail.

As the weeks passed, Sara's health began to decline. One day, as I was passing through the lobby, I saw her sitting by herself in the women's section. I knew she hadn't been well lately and went over to ask how she was feeling. She had been to see the doctor that morning, but it "really wasn't any use. I take all these pills, but I don't feel any better. I've been so sick and weak these last few days." She got up from her chair and I accompanied her upstairs. As we went toward the elevator I placed my arm supportively around her shoulders, but she moved away, saying she didn't want all those people in the lobby to see me helping her like that. She didn't want anyone to know something was wrong with her.

Several weeks later I dropped by her apartment. I noticed that the door was open to provide some cross-ventilation on the hot, smoggy day. Her room was neat and clean although she told me she had been in bed for two weeks. She talked about the kind of help she was getting from her friends in the building: "Aida, Jean, and Marian—anytime I'm sick like this they come in and help me. They do my shopping, and one woman that I hardly even know came over the other night and gave me a rub-down. Now wasn't that nice?" A tiny woman with brightly dyed auburn hair came into the room. She had come by to pick up the washing. Sara thanked her profusely, to which the woman replied that, after all, it was only what Sara deserved. Directing her remarks to me, she added, "She's helped out enough people around here." After her friend had gone, Sara related to me how her good friend Bill came in every night to visit. "He usually watches television and sometimes stays until ten. But if I'm not feeling well, he will go home earlier. He cooks my supper and tidies up for me. He's a lot fussier about housekeeping than me and can't stand it when my place is messy."

Two weeks passed and I ran into Sara as she was getting off the elevator on her way to the bingo game. I was surprised to see her up, but she was determined to go to the game regardless of how badly she was feeling. I noticed she was wearing unusually heavy makeup; her lipstick was a bright red and her cheeks were heavily rouged. As we were talking, another woman came by and mentioned she was glad to see Sara because some people down in the lobby said that she had been taken to the hospital. Sara was immediately incensed. "Wouldn't you know it! Those people down there make these things up and don't tell the truth about anything." Taking the arm of another woman who was passing by, she proceeded down the hall to the bingo game that was about to begin. I noticed that her progress was slow and unsteady.

On another occasion soon afterward I saw Sara sitting with a friend in the lobby, waiting for the mail. As I went over to say hello, I noticed again that she seemed to have taken unusual care with her appearance. She was wearing an attractive pants suit with matching shoes and a heavy string of beads. Her hair was neatly coiffured, her makeup carefully applied. When I complimented her on how nice she looked, she seemed pleased and said she was feeling better. There was something in her manner, however, that gave me the impression that her seeming brightness took considerable effort. As I looked more closely, I could see her face was pale and drawn under the heavy coat of powder.

Soon after this encounter Sara had a heart seizure and was hospitalized for two weeks. As I came through the lobby, Charles Mason, who can always be depended on to give me the latest news, said that several days ago Sara had signed herself out of the hospital and returned against her doctor's orders. Later that morning I went up to visit her.

As soon as I was settled in a chair beside her bed, she began complaining about the poor treatment she had received in the hospital. They wanted her to go to a nursing home to recuperate, but she decided to return home. She had been to those places and considered them one step away from the morgue. Her friends and Bill were still helping her and she felt much better at home. "You die in those other places, and I'm not ready for that yet." She went on to describe how Bill had been waiting for her outside when she arrived by taxi from the hospital. "When he helped me out, I had my arms full of clothes, and another guy standing there asked if we were going to call it Sara or Bill." We both laughed, and Sara went on about Bill's concern for her. "And while I was away he looked after my canary. He took the cage over to his apartment and fed it every day."

Our talk turned to the circumstances surrounding her recent hospitalization. The heart attack occurred several blocks away from the St. Regis, and she had to lean against the side of a building to keep from falling down. "Then I tried to walk back because I was determined to make it on my own. But I couldn't, and luckily this man I knew came down the street and helped me. Then we called an ambulance and they took me to the hospital, where I had all those tests. But I know they can't do anything more for me and I'm better off here."

A few weeks after this conversation I was in the manager's office when Bill, Sara's close friend, came to the door, looking upset and leaning heavily on his cane. Quietly he said that he thought Sara was dead. "I was just up there and she doesn't seem to move. I was cleaning her room for about an hour and she just lay on the bed with her face to the wall. I thought she was asleep. I didn't want to wake her up but I did go over after a while to take off her glasses. Then I saw she didn't seem to be breathing." He sat down and we offered some words of comfort.

The manager called the ambulance rescue service, and we both went up to Sara's apartment to see what could be done until the rescue team arrived. Bill, feeling too upset to go with us, said he'd stay where he was. Sara was lying in bed with a blanket tucked around her, eyes open. There was no pulse. Within twenty minutes the medical team arrived and confirmed that Sara was dead. The manager then told me I could leave, that the necessary details would be taken care of. Once the legitimate authorities had arrived, I was an outsider without official status, and my presence seemed to be in violation of the ritual circumstances of death.

Within a half hour Sara's body was removed from the building. Later, in the lobby, everyone seemed to be talking quietly about this sad event. Sara was well known and her death had some significance. Expressions of regret were mingled with attempts to provide reassuring interpretations of what had happened. One woman told me that Bill wanted to keep Sara's canary because it was all he had to remember her by. Another, who had known her closely for several years, thought it fortunate Sara was able to die in her own room instead of some nursing home where nobody really cares about you.

Shaken by the events of the day, I sunk into profound tiredness driving home. It was a relief to enter my own house and get involved in preparing dinner for my family. The world of the St. Regis seemed far away.

Conclusion

Although varying in level of physical decline and ability to control the circumstances of their lives, Armen, Miriam and Sara shared a determination to remain in their rooms and avoid confinement in a medical setting. For all three, living in the St. Regis proved advantageous as their need for care increased. Although lacking in kin and friendship networks, Armen Saroyan succeeded in securing the assistance of staff and neighbors in meeting daily maintenance needs. In spite of a terminal illness he was able to remain until close to his death. Circumstances were less kind to Miriam Davis. Growing blindness, gastrointestinal problems, and general physical decline limited her capacity to care for herself. Although she received some assistance from other residents that extended her ability to remain at home, Miriam became increasingly vulnerable to custodial care and eventually lost her apartment. In contrast, Sara Ross was able to retain residential status until her death because of the assistance of her devoted friends in the building.

The personal histories of these residents will undoubtedly arouse feelings of compassion in those who define successful aging in terms of comfortable incomes, warm surroundings, and close ties to families and friends. But for these determined survivors accustomed to limited resources and a single lifestyle, definitions of successful living primarily entail the preservation of personal independence in familiar surroundings, and this is the criterion we need to use in evaluating the viability of life at places like the St. Regis, which, for many, are home.

Chapter 8

What Can Be Done

"This place here, this building—it's the last hole," Harold Willis remarked on one occasion during my final days at the St. Regis. Initially I would have taken this statement as a negative evaluation of the quality of community life, as typifying alienation in an impersonal urban world that offered little and demanded much to survive. After months of intensive involvement in their daily lives I came to understand that for many, such comments reflected a realistic assessment of available living alternatives in the downtown area, where they preferred to remain.

During the last six months of my investigation, I asked fifty-seven tenants, forty-one men and sixteen women, the following question: "Given similar situations in terms of subsidized rent and comparable living quarters, would you consider moving to another part of Los Angeles?" Only five men and three women gave affirmative responses, and the most frequent reason for wanting to move was concern over high crime rates. Fully 83 percent of the men and 62 percent of the women wanted to remain because of nearby friends, economic advantages, close proximity to services, and territorial feelings based on long-term residence. Such responses and similar attitudes expressed by other residents during many informal encounters demonstrate that residence in the St. Regis was more generally perceived as a matter of conscious choice than of entrapment. To remain independent in familiar surroundings was the ultimate goal of many of these men and women who were struggling against difficult odds. This is why many can be called "determined survivors."

The problem, then, becomes one of determining what resources are necessary to sustain familiar lifestyles and enable access to supportive assistance in time of need. At the St. Regis, age homogeneity, physical proximity, and similarity of concerns result in a "consciousness of kind" that provides the basis for assistance exchanges compatible with established values and preferences. Being aided by similar others is minimally threatening to self-esteem. Maintaining reciprocity in helping transactions extends the availability of help: residents do not become indebted to one another and can avoid unwanted affective involvement. Survival, not sociable, concerns are the dominant features of communal life, and reciprocal aid transactions provide an important form of social insurance against loss of independence.

Negative attitudes toward confinement in long-term care facilities are universal, and "running away" from medical facilities is a frequent occurrence. From the residents' perspective, going into a hospital setting is synonymous with embarking on the death and dying process, and this view often conforms to reality. Given limited income, few significant others, and little hope for ultimate recovery, remaining in the St. Regis and depending on neighbors, friends, and staff for help is the best of possible alternatives.

Yet in spite of the benefits that collective living under these circumstances provides, there are also deficits. Security arrangements are inadequate for the high crime rates in the area and the vulnerability of frail tenants to assault and robbery. Informal support systems and protective measures undertaken by residents themselves are limited, and needs often exceed personal capacities. Assistance is not uniformly available. Individuals vary in their coping abilities, and when their strategies prove insufficient in the face of failing health and limited resources, some must pay a heavy price. These deficits underline the importance of intervention to strengthen existing natural helping networks and reduce the burdens of self-care.

Social Planning

A close fit between environmental characteristics and personal needs and preferences is an essential component of the well-being and adaptive capacity of elderly people (Kahana 1982; Lawton et al. 1980). But maintaining optimal person–environment congruence is constrained by existing choices in living arrangements, limited income, the unpredictable nature of health losses in old age, and the reluctance of some older people to use community or on-site services because of personal values stressing independence and self-sufficiency. In a needs assessment survey conducted among 154 residents of an age-segregated congregate apartment project in Philadelphia, Ehrlich et al. (1982) found that 95 percent reported they had little interest in obtaining assistance from community agencies. Although 20 percent of the residents were identified as needing aid in daily maintenance tasks, slightly less than half of this group made use of on-site supportive services implemented on their behalf.

A complication in matching residents' needs to available services is that dependency increases over time. Although advancing age alone is not an accurate predictor of functional levels, service needs of tenants will become more extensive with length of residence. In a definitive paper on the consequences of changing dependency and service needs in planned housing for the elderly, Lawton et al. (1980) describe several options available to administrators. The "constant environment" model seeks to preserve a fixed level of functional independence among the resident population by requiring incoming residents to meet certain standards of self-care and by terminating residential eligibility when capacity declines. Given the restricted choices in living arrangements for many of the inner city aged, such policies increase the likelihood of premature admission to long-term care facilities. An alternate option is the "accommodating environment" model, whereby residents experiencing increasing impairments are allowed to remain as long as skilled nursing care is not required. Supportive services are gradually introduced to match the needs of marginal tenants. Admission requirements are also relaxed so that the functional capacities of incoming residents begin to match those of current residents.

But those considering various administrative strategies must attend as well to the social characteristics and personal views of the recipients. Because of the diversity in life circumstances and individual attributes that characterize the older population, optimal supportive arrangements for some may be dysfunctional for others. To elderly people who value self-reliant lifestyles, formal programs such as housekeeping assistance and meal preparation may constitute a threat to independent functioning and symbolize an unacceptable trajectory of decline. Ehrlich and associates (1982) propose a third model, the "balanced environment" model, that stresses the importance of reducing perceived environmental change by encouraging peer-oriented, reciprocal networks as a viable alternative to bureaucratic intervention. These informal support systems make assistance available in ways that are less damaging to self-esteem and assumptions about autonomous functioning.

The provision of formal services, while critically important in many instances, is only a partial solution to meeting residents' needs. Within the bureaucratic framework, reciprocity on the part of aid receivers is usually reduced to compliance with a rigid set of eligibility criteria. In contrast, horizontal exchanges among status equals involving expectations of repayment not only are congruent with important values of self-sufficiency and a dislike for indebtedness but also result in the creation of a more reliable network of relationships (Suttles and Street 1970). These benefits assume even greater importance in settings where social relations are constrained at best. Thus programs that emulate and enhance natural helping networks not only have a greater chance of success but also contribute to the development of group cohesiveness that in the long run increases the availability of assistance.

Intervention Strategies

The preservation of perceived independence can be fostered by services that use the talents and skills of the residents. Some can be trained as in-house peer counselors who provide empathic understanding for those in need and assistance in referrals to outside agencies; committees can be organized to check periodically on reclusive tenants and those known to be seriously ill. At the St. Regis a few residents provided maintenance assistance in return for a few dollars; these kinds of arrangements can be systematized in more dependable ways. One possibility is a central registration service that lists those willing to provide housekeeping help and perform errands in return for small fees.

Marketlike transactions in daily living needs can increase the availability of goods at affordable prices. Former occupational skills can be used in providing handyman services such as repairing small electrical appliances, mending furniture, and altering clothing. Payment can be in money or through a point system in which credits for services rendered offset services received. A thrift center can be set up periodically so that used clothing, personal bric-a-brac, and household goods can be traded and sold.

At the St. Regis, for example, twice a year in the recreation room there is a successful rummage sale of used clothing, household appliances, kitchenware, books, and small pieces of furniture, either donated by tenants or unclaimed personal effects of deceased tenants. The profits are used by the Senior Citizens' Club to fund community activities such as the holiday dinners. These sales are well attended by residents and by elderly people living on the outside who take advantage of the reasonable prices. Articles made by the Arts and Crafts Club are also placed on sale at the monthly coffee parties. Club members set up an attractive display on a table in the main lobby and diligently persuade passersby to purchase their goods. Christmas decorations, potholders, antiqued plaques, and costume jewelry are quickly disposed of in transactions characterized by spirited bargaining. Even though the small profits are used to buy craft materials and refreshments for meetings, the sellers appreciate receiving money in return for their efforts.

Although problems of victimization occur at all societal levels and the burden of change should not be placed on those who are at greatest risk, safety programs that use the capacities of residents who are willing to become involved can be a valuable adjunct to existing formal and informal protective strategies. Residents can be organized to provide escort services to the bank when social security checks arrive. Tenant advocacy groups can work with management and local police on crime prevention programs and to obtain greater protection in the downtown streets.

Residents might also assist in monitoring alarm systems, emergency hot lines, and electronic surveillance devices.

Some tenants may be able to function, on a paid or volunteer basis, in a capacity similar to that of a doorman or concierge. Traditionally, doormen fulfill numerous gatekeeping and caretaking functions including screening unidentified people wishing to gain admittance, hailing taxis, watching packages, passing on messages, providing assistance when keys are lost, and exchanging friendly conversation. The concierges of France typically occupy a ground floor apartment and act as a resident representative of management. In the St. Regis the informal lobby squad performs an important surveillance function, and the security guard provides some assistance that exceeds formally defined duties. There is room, however, for an able resident to function in a doormanlike capacity. Equipped with emblems of office such as a badge or uniform and a beeper to summon help if necessary, this person could be stationed close to the main entrance to monitor incoming traffic and assist those entering and leaving the building. In settings where staff members are not in residence, a tenant could also assume tasks similar to those of a concierge and handle complaints about needed building repairs, quarrels between neighbors, and lost keys, as well as call the police or medical teams in emergencies.

Furthermore, in residential facilities such as the St. Regis, planned programs need to be directed toward survival concerns rather than recreational interests. Structured opportunities for sociable interaction are important, but at the St. Regis many prefer to satisfy recreational and friendship needs on the outside. Speakers on topics such as defensive measures in the city streets, social security regulations, Medicare provisions, nutrition, health needs, and drug usage may elicit greater interest and result in the largest turnouts.

Overall, services not congruent with the perceived needs and value orientations of the recipients have limited success. Service delivery programs thus need to be geared to the belief systems and informal helping modes occurring naturally among residents. As Clark (1971) says, "If planned programs can be

constructed to emulate or develop these spontaneous arrangements among people, they are likely to be accepted and effective"
(64). This principle is applicable not only to services for the
aged living in planned housing but to the aged living independently in the community and to other groups struggling to
maintain viable roles in the face of diminishing capacity to survive independently.

Conclusion

Although this study focused on individual and collective survival
strategies in one age-segregated housing complex for the inner
city elderly, similarities in life circumstances make it possible to
generalize the findings to other settings providing collective living for the aged and for marginal members of society. Some features of group life may differ in privately owned SRO hotels and
age-integrated planned housing because of the presence of families and younger people. Also, this investigation was limited to a
largely Caucasian population, so the conclusions may require
modification for ethnic groups. Jackson (1980), for example, has
shown that Asians view the aging process and responsibilities of
family members in significantly different ways, which would
affect both the degree to which kin networks are relied on for
assistance and the attitudes toward living in retirement facilities. Given the increasing numbers of minority-group people in
many central city areas, social planners will need to consider the
unique needs of ethnically diverse populations. Yet poverty,
health losses, the lack of meaningful employment, limited social
networks, and substandard living conditions are common denom-
inators in the struggle to exist regardless of ethnicity and how
long one has lived. Viewing the ways in which the St. Regis
tenants cope with daily survival challenges provides guidelines
for determining how many disadvantaged people construct and
maintain adaptive strategies in their efforts to avoid custodial
confinement and remain on their own.

Our society is committed to the principle of enabling diverse
groups to participate in the American dream of the good life in

ways that respect individual needs and preferences. Although the living patterns of many who are designated as "problems" do not conform to socially approved norms, the obligation remains to respect their right to self-determination in their surroundings. The challenge to social scientists and officials concerned with the public welfare is thus to respect the views of people living marginal existences and to enable them, if such is their choice, to pursue their chosen lifestyles by providing them with supportive arrangements that ameliorate the degrading conditions associated with poverty and inadequate housing.

As Harold Willis says, "Just because people get old doesn't mean they change. They're what they've been most of their lives. This world has in it a lot of different types. In fact a lot of older people have the same problems as younger people—a lot of blacks have the same problems as whites. But you have to get in and understand the people according to the way they are and how they are living. If you come in with just a certain way of looking at things, then that's all you're going to see. Then you miss a lot that's going on that might be more important or more true."

Appendix

In the Field

The findings of a study do not exist independent of the methods by which they are produced. The investigator inevitably becomes a part of the social context in ways that critically influence the processes of data collection and interpretation of the findings.[1] Formalized accounts that neglect these considerations reflect a consistency of participation that is not in accordance with existing reality and ignores the humanity of the observer. These concerns are particularly relevant to the method of participant observation in which the researcher becomes involved "in the daily life of the people under study. . . . observing things that happen, listening to what is said and questioning people over some length of time" (Becker and Greer 1957:28).[2] Therefore, the validity of recorded findings depends on the inclusion of subjective responses to given events and on assessments of the varying ways in which the field worker is perceived by group members.

In the discussion that follows, I present a naturalistic account of my field work experiences at the St. Regis in which I emphasize the reflexive and interactive components that critically influenced information-gathering processes and analytical findings. Currently there is a growing interest in studies concerned with the quality of life experienced by the elderly in age-segregated surroundings. I also hope my analysis will provide a sort of anticipatory socialization for those who venture into similar settings.

Data Collection and Analysis

My involvement in the setting began in December 1975 and lasted for two and a half years. During this time I was in the building at least two or three days a week, and on frequent occa-

sions I made additional trips to attend meetings and social gatherings. I also varied my hours to observe social behavior during
the morning, afternoon, and evening hours. On two occasions I
was absent for a one-month interval because of family vacations.

My primary methods of data collection were participant observation through informal direct encounters with residents and
staff; the use of secondary sources such as Housing Authority records and statistical information from community agencies; and
indirect measures such as a content analysis of the main bulletin
board and noting variations in lobby seating patterns.[3] Most
information I obtained informally from residents-at-large, and
while in the setting I came to know over one hundred of them,
many on a first-name basis. Among these acquaintances, more intimate and extended contacts came about with twenty-seven persons. I have altered names and other kinds of identifying information to protect the anonymity of those with whom I became
involved, but I have endeavored none the less to adhere closely to
the actual circumstances of their lives and reflect accurately the
situations that occurred.

Observations, I systematically recorded in detailed field notes,
which were the main basis for analysis. I did not use a tape re-
corder during actual conversations, but on the long drive home
I routinely tape-recorded impressions and experiences while
they were still fresh in my mind. Initially I attempted to record
everything that occurred, but after six months, I began to observe more systematically as my awareness of the important ways
in which age-segregated living contributed to survival capacities increased.

One of the major advantages in conducting observations over
an extended period is the opportunity to reorient research concerns according to a growing understanding of the nature of
group interaction and to test out tentative assumptions and hy-
potheses while the study is in progress (Becker and Greer 1957).
Gradually, major topics such as assistance behavior and safety
concerns began to emerge as highly important features of communal life, and related details could be cross-referenced with field
notes that I had recorded in chronological order. For example,

when it occurred to me that the motivation for helping was primarily utilitarian, based on notions of reciprocity, rather than altruistic, I was able to catalog examples of assistance behavior according to type and then cross-reference them by page number with the master set of field notes. The fact that I was still present in the setting provided opportunities to test out this assumption by systematically asking those involved in helping transactions if friendship was a determining factor.

After I had been in the setting for a year, I was able to gain limited access to Housing Authority records with the understanding that I would respect the confidential nature of the files. I spent many hours perusing old records and index cards and as a result was able to derive calculations concerning population characteristics that supported a number of observational findings. I obtained additional insights from a logbook in which other counselors recorded their experiences and observations.

I also used several indirect measures such as counting the number of people in the lobby area at different times of the day to determine the lobby's importance as a focal point for community interaction and observing the kinds of refuse left in containers in the lobby and lounge. Several notices were posted asking residents to refrain from eating and drinking in these areas so as not to attract ants and roaches, but few seemed to be observing these directives, judging from the food wrappers, empty bottles, and other kinds of refuse I observed. This seeming disregard of Housing Authority regulations was an indicator of subtle but pervasive patterns of tenant resistance to the encroachment of bureaucratic demands on independent behavioral styles.

The investigation of any complex social grouping always involves the impossibility of being universally present, and the observer must of necessity rely on descriptions by others when significant events occur during periods of absence. I was fortunate in this regard. The counselors who worked with me provided insightful descriptions of their own experiences and of situations I was personally unable to observe. Two men and several women residents also functioned as surrogate observers and never failed to inform me about important happenings such as community reac-

tions to several fires that broke out in the hotel next door and instances of criminal assaults.

Generalizing from the viewpoints of a few is questionable according to the canons of scientific fact finding; yet several studies
done by Campbell (1955) and Vidal and Shapiro (1955) indicate
a close correspondence between the attitudes of a selected group
of informants and findings on the same issues obtained from more
traditional survey methods. Admittedly problems of bias and selective observing exist, but the effects can be controlled to some
extent by maintaining an awareness of character idiosyncracies
and by comparing descriptions of the same event with those given
by others.

It would be inaccurate for me to claim that the residents I
relied on gave me wholly objective accountings, for like anyone
else, they have biased opinions and observe in selective ways. But
as I came to know them more intimately, I tried to take these aspects into account and tested out their observations with other
tenants. Obtaining information from informants does not meet
the specifications of statistical fact finding, but in view of the
qualitative methods of inquiry I was using and my inability to be
in the building at certain times, this strategy was advantageous
and resulted in the collection of data that would otherwise have
been unobtainable.

One of the major difficulties facing the participant observer is
the need to establish contact with representative members of the
population under study. Unlike other types of research, sampling
in participant observation is usually carried out during the course
of the research in relation to a developing understanding of important topics. There is, however, always the danger of deriving generalizations based on contacts with those groups who are
most accessible.

In the St. Regis there were members of some groupings who
were largely unavailable to me because of their lifestyles and the
fact that I was a woman. Some residents who were chronic alcoholics preferred to remain secluded in their rooms and only emerged
to purchase needed food and replenish their liquor supplies. My
efforts to establish sustained contact with this group were usually

unsuccessful, for I was often perceived as some type of official who might report to management on the extent of their drinking activities. It was also difficult to become acquainted with transients who would surreptitiously leave before their rent was due. In addition, access to some male-oriented activities such as drinking at the corner bar and going to the race track was limited by my gender. There was also the problem of needing to consider the possibility of sex bias in data obtained from a population where men outnumbered women three to one.

The length of time I was in the setting and the large number of contacts I was able to make functioned to counteract many of these difficulties. From other residents I was able to gather details about the lifestyles of those who were long-term drinkers. Although I did not personally accompany racing enthusiasts to the track, I obtained information about these activities through informal conversations with those who were involved, and I learned to appreciate the intricate reasoning used in picking a sure winner. I also purposely expanded the number of contacts with male residents, and among those I knew more intimately, 65 percent were men.

Field Work Relationships

In any social setting the identity ascribed to the researcher is a product of self-definitions, personality dispositions, roles that are familiar and meaningful to group members, and situational circumstances (Johnson 1975). Admittedly, the mutually constituted images of one another that the observer and the observed hold tend to stabilize over time, and as the months went by, I was predominantly seen as a helping person and friend. But the existence of variation in the roles I came to occupy and the reasons why this occurred became a substantive part of the social reality I was investigating.[4]

Although the many services I performed fostered my acceptance among community members, my counseling role entailed a number of problems in relation to my research activities. There were many days in which details associated with the handling of concrete requests necessitating paper work and phone calls consumed important hours that could have been more profitably spent on research-oriented matters. It was often difficult to lead conversations into broader areas of community interaction when an incomprehensible medical bill was the prime concern. Thus I found myself caught in both a moral and a tactical dilemma. Given my own values and the reality of extensive needs, it was personally impossible for me not to provide aid where I could. Furthermore, if I restricted the amount of assistance I was giving, I would be violating already established expectations of residents and staff, which could jeopardize my standing in the community. Consequently I was placed in the complicated position of having to integrate two roles that were in some ways diametrically opposed. But having already committed myself and faced with the reality of extensive needs for assistance, there was little I could do but maneuver within already established parameters.

Although the majority of my contacts were friendly, a few people thought I was a covert investigator for the Housing Authority and others saw me as an unwanted intruder. These reactions were prevalent during the first few months. Some reclusive tenants had no idea who I was or my reasons for being in the building. Several asked if I had been sent by the office to see if they were still able to take care of themselves; one woman wondered if I had come by to see whether or not her apartment was clean, and others simply closed the door when I stopped by to introduce myself. Initially I was hurt by these apparent rejections but later came to realize that I did not occupy some kind of privileged position that obligated residents to become involved with me. To some I was an unknown outsider who did not possess rights of entry into their private worlds.

Some tenants tried to make use of my connections with management to expedite requests for room transfers and furniture repairs. In other instances I was hustled for money, as in the following situation: One hot, smoggy day I was sharing a bottle of beer with John Thompson, a heavily built, congenial man who admitted to the age of 84. The conversation turned to horse racing and he described in detail his foolproof betting system. "But I need a partner," he stated. "A social security check doesn't go far, and if you've got some spare money, maybe you'd like to go in with me. I almost always win, and we'd split the winnings fifty-fifty." I pleaded abject poverty, but he remained unconvinced as he continued to elaborate on his betting expertise for the next hour.

Another group of tenants viewed me primarily as a companion and someone who could be entrusted with confidential information that would not become part of the gossip system. Most of these relationships developed within a framework of social visiting and recreational outings. For these residents my position as an outsider possessed what Merton (1947) has referred to as "stranger value." My nonresidential status and the limited amount of time I spent in the setting made me a safer person to associate with, and complaints about management and other residents could be shared without fear of reprisal.

This group typically distanced themselves from the rest of the population, whom they often referred to in derogatory terms. Instead, they preferred to develop social contacts and fulfill recreational needs on the outside. I, however, was someone who was different. Relating to a person who was younger and in more advantaged circumstances seemed to reinforce this needed sense of difference in self-enhancing ways. To them I was a concerned and interested friend who was willing to sit for hours listening to stories of past experiences, exchanging opinions about political events, and expressing sympathy about personal concerns.

Some of the women regarded me as a friendly visitor who was available for lunch and recreational excursions. Intimate conversations were often held over cups of coffee and a sandwich in individual apartments or during outings to nearby parks. Several initiated me into the techniques of bargain shopping in downtown department stores, and others took me to meals in nearby neighborhood nutrition sites. Similarities in marital status provided the basis for sharing common experiences in familial roles. Many had raised children, and together we discussed the joys and sorrows of parenthood. The opinion was frequently expressed that today's younger generation had not learned to appreciate the importance of thrift and hard work—one had to go through the experience of a depression to know the real meaning of hard times.

In some instances the fact that I was often twenty-five years younger resulted in the development of quasi-parental situations in which a few women who were isolated from their families assumed a protective, proprietary interest in my personal affairs. Ellen Williams, for example, a seventy-year-old Caucasian woman who had little contact with her three grown children living on the East Coast, became increasingly attached to me and frequently issued directives regarding the conduct of my family affairs and academic career. She strongly disagreed with my desire for a second career and felt that a middle-aged woman such as myself should stay at home with her husband and family. "Behind every successful man there's a good woman—and that's where you should be," she often stated, invoking the Bible as a persuasive reference. She became more demanding in her requests for my time and assistance and would be upset if I was unable to comply because of commitments to other tenants.

I was usually treated with respect and consideration by the male tenants, but a few situations did occur in which sexual advances were explicit. In the following situation, a joking reference to my family proved to be an effective way of handling the encounter. One day when I was waiting for the elevator on the sixth floor, a man who had just moved in came up to me and wanted to know how much it would cost if I went with him to his room. He was obviously very drunk, and I jokingly cautioned him that he wouldn't want to get involved with me because of my ten children. "You I can't afford," he replied, and continued down the hall.

Management of Personal Differences

Characteristics such as age, marital status, socioeconomic position, and gender significantly influence the kinds of relationships that develop between the researcher and the observed group. When I began the study I was concerned that being economically comfortable, substantially younger, and married might negatively affect my ability to establish rapport, but as I became more intimately involved with the tenants, these personal attributes seemed to work in my favor. Many said they enjoyed being around someone who was younger because they wearied of seeing wrinkled faces and graying hair. And the fact I was married and had children was advantageous. I often brought my daughters, aged ten and fourteen, to help out on social occasions. This involvement of family members was positively received and seemed to be interpreted as an indication of my liking and respect for the residents.

Differences in financial status aroused the greatest feelings of discomfort on my part. Initially I avoided wearing expensive clothes and was careful not to talk about my comfortable home or costly social outings, but I came to realize that this behavior only reinforced my own feelings of difference. Respect for the values and lifestyles of groups substantially different in background characteristics is more effectively communicated by an honest presentation of self than by conscious efforts to "come down to their level." The assumption of behavior that does not conform to the researchers real self can also obstruct observational capacities because of the heavy drain on psychic energy that can be involved. In my own experience, an honest recognition of personal differences instead of awkward attempts to disguise status dissimilarities proved to be effective in a place where "being a phony" was widely condemned.

In a setting heavily dominated by men, I found that a willingness to participate in joking exchanges often characterized by suggestive undertones was another way to manage existing differences. The frequency of this style of talk alerted me to its significance for communication. The following example took place during my first week and was typical of these kinds of encounters. As I was entering the lobby I stopped to say hello to Harold and John, who were occupying their customary chairs. Harold asked what a fine looking lady like myself was doing in this part of town and how come my husband trusted me out alone like this. I smiled and said that my husband trusted me out alone just as much as I trusted him. We all laughed and then John alluded to the fact that he had been a fast one with the ladies in his day. But now he was too old. Consequenty my husband didn't have to worry about him. I then put in, "You are only as old as you feel." He winked and we were all smiling as I left to go upstairs. Reacting with humor in this instance helped to bridge status differences by invoking what Goffman (1967) has referred to as "symmetrical familiarity." Suggestive remarks have a leveling effect because of the presumption of intimacy that comments of this nature imply. Thus a form of equivalence, however fleeting, is established that enables the interaction to proceed more smoothly in face-saving ways.

Joking exchanges with residents frequently touched on age differences and, with some, assumed a ritualistic character that served to limit further conversational involvement. When entering and leaving the building I routinely passed by several men who, although friendly, politely resisted attempts to enter into prolonged talk. I was not part of their male-oriented world, which was dominated by an interest in horse racing and other kinds of sporting events. One man, who was in his late seventies and an inveterate devotee of horse racing, would invariably make the following remarks when I paused to say hello: "You sure look good today. When I see you coming I say to myself, 'Here comes a young girl who looks sixteen.'" In response I would usually say that a remark like that was good to hear and I felt he didn't look a day over twenty-one himself. Invariably we would laugh and feel comfortable in the familiarity of these exchanges that rarely proceeded beyond this point. A tacit recognition of the differences in our ages was accomplished and a sense of closure was operative in which subsequent remarks seemed inappropriate.

Thus the use of humor in this setting possessed a serious character and facilitated interaction in important ways. Joking comments provided a way of acknowledging existing differences while at the same time enabling a comfortable framework within which dissimilarities could be handled. Failure to respond in kind would have resulted in disruptive consequences with a negative affect on the rapport I was working to establish.

Special Problems

Working continuously in a setting over a long period, the researcher inevitably becomes more intimately involved with some members. This involvement has particular consequences in a setting with large concentrations of low-income elderly people where material deprivation, social isolation, and frequent exposure to death and dying can result in unanticipated levels of emotional involvement. Little has been written about this problem, and workers entering such communities can be ill prepared. Failure to recognize these personal reactions denies the humanity of the observer and results in an overly formalized accounting of field work experiences.

In the St. Regis where loneliness and the need for sociable contacts can be extreme, remaining emotionally uninvolved was not possible for me. On one hand, I was drawn into close affiliation with some residents because of empathic reactions to their needs. On the other, it was necessary for me to learn to cope with grieving responses resulting from serious illness and death. Thus the tension between rapport and objectivity was compounded by the strain between the formation of intimate ties and fears of loss.[5]

In the early stages of the study I was unprepared to cope with my grief when several people I became fond of during the first year died. The demise of one man in particular affected me deeply. We had shared many pleasant hours together in which he talked at length about his personal beliefs and his satisfaction with his past life. He died suddenly of a heart attack alone in his room and was discovered within a few hours by a neighbor who became concerned when he didn't answer the phone. His death was not unexpected—he suffered from a chronic heart condition and was eighty-six years old—but I reacted strongly and, because of my grief, found it difficult to function in the researcher role. I should have visited the setting as soon as possible to investigate collective reactions to the passing of someone who was well known and respected, but to have done so in this instance would have violated my personal convictions of propriety. I was emotionally unable to reenter the building until a week later. By that time, reactions to his death had lost their immediacy and had probably undergone alterations in the processes of communication.

In all honesty, I was never able to remain detached or uninvolved when residents I knew became seriously ill or died. I continued to grieve on a number of occasions, but repeated exposure did increase my ability to accept the inevitability of death as a built-in feature of a retirement community. I no longer ran away when a death occurred, and I lost my sense of vulturelike intent when faced with the need to explore members' reactions. I came to realize that this kind of information would help others involved in working with older populations to understand the meanings attached to the death and dying process in similar settings. On a more personal level, too, I became better prepared to face my own mortality.

In general, this study can be viewed as partly descriptive and partly analytical. The extensive use of case histories and anecdotal evidence typifying the lifestyles, personal experiences, and attitudes of the residents toward many facets of collective living in this setting, enables the reader to perceive the quality of community life from the perspectives of those who are directly involved. On an analytical level, I arrange empirical data in the context of theoretical constructs that best seem to interpret the evidence. The method of participant observation does not enable me to provide conclusive proof for all of the conclusions, but I know of no other strategy that is better suited to the task of getting close to the daily lives of group members.

Notes

Introduction

1. An information paper published by the U.S. Senate Committee on Aging (1978) defines SRO facilities as: "(a) furnished rooms with or without self-contained bathrooms; (b) usually without kitchens (may be communal); (c) some management services (desks, linens, housekeeping); (d) permanent occupants (at least half the tenants); (e) commercial establishment (neither subsidized or licensed for institutional care); (f) frequently the physical facility is old or deteriorated with systems needing replacement; (g) usually these facilities are located in commercial areas" (6).

2. Wirth (1938), for example, argued that the segmented character of large city populations and the transitory nature of social relations resulted in the loss of "the sense of participation that comes with living in an integrated society" (3)—a condition analogous to the Durkeimian concept of anomie. Increased social isolation and perceptions of powerlessness were the consequences of these kinds of conditions.

3. To test Wirth's (1938) urban-alienation hypothesis, Fischer (1973) conducted a secondary analysis of three large surveys based on sample populations in both the United Kingdom and the United States. Using two dimensions of alienation (powerlessness and social isolation), Fischer found no significant correlation between size of community and feelings of powerlessness as defined in terms of self-perceptions of personal competence. Fischer did find, however, a small but statistically significant relation between urbanism and social isolation as measured in terms of self-perceived degrees of trust or mistrust toward others. The author surmised that this latter finding was more adequately explained by the pluralistic character of urban populations than by sheer size.

Urbanites could be fully integrated into their own groups and yet be mistrustful of outsiders, a more complex situation than the type of social isolation emphasized in the original hypothesis.

4. An example of this can also be found in Shapiro's (1971) description of the types of tenants occupying SRO buildings in New York City: "They are, in effect, the slum hotels providing transient and permanent homes for alcoholics, addicts, prostitutes, petty criminals, the indigent chronically ill, the mentally retarded adult, the mentally ill and the elderly—all people who cannot adequately care for themselves in the larger society" (15).

Chapter 1

1. To protect the identity of the residents, all names have been changed.

2. At the time of this investigation, the suggested donation for elderly people attending such nutrition programs primarily financed by the federal government under the Older Americans Act was sixty-five cents. Means tests to determine financial eligibility were not and are not involved. In 1983 the average donation increased to one dollar.

3. These inspections are conducted several times a year to determine need for roach control and to meet fire-inspection regulations. The rental lease agreement also requires residents to maintain reasonable housekeeping standards.

4. Between 1970 and 1977 the number of women tenants declined by only 4 percent, although with some small racial differences, as Tables 1.5 and 1.6 indicate (the numbers of Caucasian women decreased by 5 percent, whereas the percentage of black women lessened only slightly). Overall, however, the distribution of men and women has tended to remain the same, and in 1977, 32 percent of incoming residents were women.

5. Parallels in marital status can also be seen in the populations of other studies of the urban elderly (Siegal 1978; Stephens 1976). In Chicago, for example, residential hotels and public housing contained disproportionate numbers of those who were divorced, separated, or never married compared with other residential sites (Bild and Havighurst 1976). Indeed these findings suggest that those without

family ties seek out such facilities, where ways of life are more congruent with solitary lifestyles.

6. Similar occupational patterns are evidenced by other studies of aged urban groups. Bild and Havighurst (1976) found that the majority of tenants in downtown residential hotels and public housing projects had been variously employed as craftsmen, clerical workers, operators, laborers, and service workers. In contrast to beliefs that occupants of downtown hotels exhibit unreliable work patterns, those living in San Diego hotels had an average job tenure of twenty-one years (Erickson and Eckert 1977).

7. In the Chicago study (Bild and Havighurst 1976), many residents of public housing also felt their needs were fairly well met and viewed themselves as better off financially than other older people. As the researchers state: "Looking on the bright side seems to be a special quality of many of the elderly revealed through this study. Often heard was. 'What's the use of complaining?' followed by enumerations of their sources of contentment and of misfortunes which had befallen a neighbor, friend or acquaintance" (35). For example, one seventy-one-year-old man who lived by himself and had never married had a monthly income of $157. Of this amount $45 was spent on rent, $90 on food, and $10 for needed clothing. He viewed his income as adequate for his needs and felt he was not deprived of any of the essentials. In contrast, those living in privately owned uptown residential hotels were less satisfied. Only 17 percent felt their needs were well covered, and about half went without necessary food and clothing. One sixty-three-year-old woman who had been divorced for a number of years received $191 a month, of which she spent $140 on rent and allocated $40 for food. A comparison of these monthly expenditures dramatically illustrates the survival advantages of subsidized rentals, which release scarce dollars for other necessities.

8. These proportions are representative of the current predominance of white elderly in many central city areas. Aged people have the lowest mobility rates of any group and tend to remain in neighborhoods where they have lived for many years (Atchley 1980). Recent figures indicate, however, that the black aged are rapidly becoming urbanized. Between 1950 and 1970 the numbers of nonwhite aged people living in inner cities increased by 17 percent (Bild and Havighurst 1976). Thus the

numbers of black and other minority-group residents in age-concentrated settings, particularly those offering subsidized rentals, should increase significantly in the near future.

9. In a longitudinal study examining changing dependency needs among residents of two congregate housing sites in Philadelphia, Lawton et al. (1980) found that the overall mean age of all tenants (including original and newly admitted residents) in both sites increased significantly over periods of twelve and seventeen years. In 1977 the average age of tenants in the two sites was 83.4 and 83.6 years. They also found noticeable declines in levels of functional health, which were accounted for by the overall aging of the resident population and the fact that incoming tenants were older and in poorer health than the original tenants. Self-selection factors were obviously operative: applicants in greater need of supportive services were more likely to apply than younger, still vigorous people.

10. In San Diego (Erickson and Eckert 1977) many have lived in the hotels for at least three years, some in the same building for over twenty years. Interesting differences are seen, however, in the Chicago study (Bild and Havighurst 1976). Although many tenants in residential hotels and public housing had lived in the same facility for some time, those in public housing exhibited significantly lower rates of population turnover (Table 1.2). Although residents in both kinds of facilities were poorer and exhibited higher levels of impairment than aged inhabitants of other residential settings included in the investigation, tenants in public housing scored lowest on both dimensions. Although the greater majority of occupants in these settings did not want to move, 83 percent of those in public housing wanted to stay compared with 74 percent in residential hotels.

Chapter 2

1. Most of my contacts were informal and nondirective. The few occasions on which I attempted to conduct more structured interviews around a particular topic of interest to me were less than satisfying, and I learned that this kind of population was wary of "investigatory talk." If my questions seemed too direct and out of line, the conversation would often be terminated with a polite excuse or an ambiguous comment like "Well, I don't know about that." Those who became closely

involved in the purposes of my study were more cooperative, but their willingness to share intimate details was only apparent after sufficient trust was established. Norms of privacy and suspicious attitudes resulting from cumulative experience with information-seeking officials did not provide the framework for asking pointed questions that exceeded expected boundaries of sociable discourse.

2. These counselors underwent a six-week training program oriented toward the needs of low-income elderly. Most were involved in graduate-level counseling programs and wanted supervised experience in working directly with an elderly population. Over a six-month period their numbers diminished to a core group of six who provided many volunteer hours of dedicated service. During the years of my study, other counselors replaced those who were unable to remain because of family, school, and job responsibilities. The number of counselors throughout remained relatively constant at around six. I remain deeply grateful for their insightful contributions to my research and their generous contributions of time and effort on behalf of the St. Regis residents.

3. The club also sponsors community holiday dinners at Thanksgiving and Christmas. These events are held in a large room in the basement that on other occasions is rented out by the private owners to different community groups. The dinners are usually well attended by over one hundred residents, and a palatable meal of turkey, cranberry sauce, mashed potatoes, assorted vegetables, and pumpkin pie is served for a nominal fee of two dollars. A few residents contribute table decorations and assist in setting the tables. I attended one Christmas dinner at which there was considerable difficulty setting up the warming tables for the prepared food catered by a nearby restaurant. Some residents complained afterward that they wanted their money back because the biscuits and potatoes were cold.

4. Other investigations also find that many of the urban elderly are less sociably inclined than other aged groups (Bild and Havighurst 1976; S. Sherman 1975a, 1975b; Stephens 1976). Erickson and Eckert (1977), for example, found that 82 percent of the elderly residents of working-class hotels in San Diego stated that they did not get together with other tenants for sociable activities.

5. In a study focusing on issues of successful community formation in age-segregated housing, Francis (1981) examined the influences of prior patterns of familial involvement and friendship networks, peer relations within the settings, and management patterns on the development of communal cohesiveness in two residential facilities for low-income elderly. The first one, located in Leeds, England, was a closely knit grouping in which innovative management policies enabled residents to participate actively in and control important areas of community life. Through a viable tenants' organization and other committees, residents planned and directed activities in religion, recreation, and assistance to members. In the second facility, situated in Cleveland, Ohio, findings contrasted. The social organization was amorphous and lacking in opportunities for participation in decision making and in planning community events. There was no intermediary group to facilitate tenant–management relations, and residents were hesitant to oppose administrative policies.

Structural features such as administrative policies in both the planning and daily operation of retirement facilities play a critical role and can inhibit the development of a cohesive community infrastructure. Such issues can make all the difference to success in adjusting to the status of old age in age-homogeneous surroundings. In spite of important differences in population characteristics between these two groups and the residents of the St. Regis, the centrally focused administrative structure of management undoubtedly discourages those possessing leadership skills and sociable inclinations from efforts to influence administrative policies.

6. Similarly, Hannerz (1969) analyzed the ways in which community life in a black ghetto neighborhood in Washington, D.C., was situationally adaptive. He pointed up the necessity for community members to possess a working knowledge of the potentials for trouble in their environment so as to cope with a world that promised little and gave even less. Residential proximity did not guarantee the formation of positive relationships. In a situation where choice of living arrangements was constrained by poverty and segregative policies, daily interaction among members also necessitated the development of strategies for avoiding those residents perceived as potentially troublesome. But

such distancing mechanisms still represented a mode of participation in the community as a whole and constituted an effective way of relating to undesirable others.

Chapter 5

1. Many elderly people in urban areas tend to underutilize community resources (Cantor 1975; Eckert 1979a; Sokolovsky and Cohen 1978). Lopata (1975) blames this lack of usage on inadequate knowledge about what services are available and lack of skill in knowing how to avail themselves of existing programs. She found that although important services such as meal delivery programs, medical facilities, and information centers were available for the urban aged in Chicago, many were either unaware of these programs or reluctant to use them. Clark (1971), however, argues that among New York's inner city aged, the lack of use results from a deep distrust. Erickson and Eckert (1977) also found that elderly residents in San Diego hotels "were . . . independent self-reliant individuals who were not dependent on public or private social services, nor had they been in the past" (446). Placing a high premium on their self-sufficiency, many in these hotels avoided using community services and instead relied on informal supportive assistance supplied by neighbors, friends, and hotel staff. Asked if they would like to receive any help, 75 percent answered no; 73 percent stated that they were not receiving any aid from agencies or community organizations.

2. Comparable findings exist in a study of retired blue-collar residents in a trailer park (S. K. Johnson 1971). In this setting, physical nearness and similarities in status provide the basis for extensive helping behavior that encompasses exchanges of food, household repairs, and assistance in housekeeping during sickness.

3. In the findings of another study concerned with the mental and physical well-being of a group of aged subjects in the San Francisco area (Clark 1971), inner city residents placed considerable emphasis on their desires for autonomy and privacy and did not want to interact frequently with their neighbors, although most stressed the importance of having someone nearby in case of emergency.

4. This was one of the important findings in Blau's study (1955) of the type of interaction occurring between sixteen agents in a federal law enforcement agency. He found that most agents preferred to turn to

each other rather than their supervisors because requesting help from those of equal status was less likely to involve admissions of incompetence.

5. A considerable body of evidence also demonstrates that the existence of opportunities for repayment increases the willingness to ask for and receive needed assistance and also enhances motivation to help others (Gergen et al. 1974; Greenberg and Shapiro 1971; Gross and Latane 1974).

6. There is also a moral character to these transactions. In his concept of distributive justice, Homans (1958) postulates that in situations where costs and rewards are perceived as being unequal, individuals will, in response to notions of fairness, strive to achieve a state of balance between the two. In a similar vein, Adams (1963) stipulates that when an imbalance exists between costs and rewards, people will experience an uncomfortable state of "inequity" that results in feelings of disturbance that can only be relieved by altering either costs or rewards in the direction of more equalized distributions.

7. Because of personal preference or lack of existing ties, many of the downtown elderly are unable to depend on immediate families or relatives for help. Many are either unmarried, separated, or divorced and without children (Bild and Havighurst 1976; S. Sherman 1975a). In the San Diego study (Erickson and Eckert 1977), between 76 and 79 percent of tenants in skid row and working-class hotels saw relatives either infrequently or never. When asked who they could rely on in case of emergency, only 8 percent of all respondents named family members.

8. In a one-month period, three desk clerks were fired for different reasons. One was providing empty rooms to prostitutes in return for a percentage of their fees; another had a background of antisocial behavior and was arrested for carrying a concealed weapon. Maids, desk clerks, and switchboard personnel often had unstable work histories and generally only stayed for short periods.

9. When this conversation took place, there were no security guards on the premises between two and eight in the morning.

10. Jesus's replacement was an Oriental man in his middle years who did not provide the same kinds of assistance. Residents who had depended on Jesus either managed for themselves or obtained the services of a Latino woman living on the outside.

11. The term *illness* in this instance refers to a variety of acute and chronic conditions that result in restricted activities and consequent deficit in self-maintenance. Examples include influenza, cardiovascular conditions, severe arthritis and rheumatism, gastrointestinal disturbances, cancer, and recuperation following surgery.

12. Obtaining housekeeping assistance from the Department of Public Social Services under present regulations is a complicated process involving confirmation of medical disability, an on-site visit by a social worker, verification of income, and locating someone willing to perform cleaning chores at minimal rates. This procedure can take four to six weeks before verification is received. Considerable paper work is also involved for the elderly recipient. He or she must keep track of the dates on which work was performed and when payments were made. Often the complications involved in obtaining this service are perceived as exceeding the advantages of added help.

13. In a study that analyzed contributions made to a campaign sponsored by the *New York Times* in which monies were solicited for one hundred needy cases, researchers found that cases of child abuse and people needing medical aid attracted the greatest number of contributions. Conversely, situations involving moral wrongdoings and mental illnesses received proportionately fewer donations. In analyzing these findings, Berkowitz (1972) concluded that when "misfortunes were attributed to the individual's own deficiencies" (104), the impetus to help declines. Similarly, in another experimentally designed study, Berkowitz and Friedman (1967) found that subjects were more inclined to provide assistance to their partners when increased dependency levels were perceived as resulting from factors beyond the individual's control. Although neither findings were directly concerned with crisis situations per se, they are helpful in indicating some of the factors affecting decisions to intervene. Determinations that the victim is at fault can also be influenced by knowledge of the person's past patterns of conduct. The greater the degree to which people possess public reputations as being chronic complainers, habitual drunks, or alarmists, the less will be the likelihood that nearby others will define the situation as one requiring immediate intervention.

14. Qualities of personal attractiveness have been found to influence the willingness of others to provide assistance (Daniels and Berkowitz

1963; Krebs 1970). In time of critical need, however, it is understandable that norms of social responsibility would supersede evaluations of individual attributes because of the negative consequences that could result if assistance were not forthcoming. Thus estimations of personal likeability would be more likely to affect decisions to provide help in situations of prolonged illness in which the consequences of noninvolvement would be less critical or immediately apparent.

Chapter 6

1. In contrast, Rainwater found that more advantaged groups were less likely to live in high-risk areas and were more inclined to view their homes as places of self-expression and more varied forms of social interaction.

2. Residents often complain, however, about the difficulties involved in obtaining repairs in a reasonable length of time. Electrical and plumbing problems usually receive quick attention, but it can take a number of months before worn-out draperies and broken furniture are replaced.

3. In a three-year participant-observer study of elderly members of an Appalachian community, Rowles (1981) focused on the significance of surveillance zones in the lives of old people living in their own homes. The visual field afforded by observation points such as windows and doors had important implications in the emergence of watchful reciprocal networks encompassing many helping activities with neighbors and also in the degree of vicarious participation in the outside world. In the design and location of housing for the elderly, the significance of surveillance zones in the lives of older people should receive greater consideration. Architectural features may inadvertently contribute to social isolation and reduced opportunities for assistance among a population who are already at risk.

4. Sommer (1969) writes that "when we understand the functions served by a given space we can predict how strongly it will be defended and the sorts of defensive tactics likely to be used" (43).

5. In their studies of territorial behavior, Lyman and Scott (1967) differentiate among three forms of territorial transgressions: (a) contamination, in which a given area is rendered impure according to the way in which it is customarily defined and used; (b) violation, which consists of

unwarranted usage of the territory; and (c) invasion, in which the physical presence of outsiders within specifically defined boundaries is viewed as potentially threatening to the welfare of the occupants. Within this theoretical framework, the presence of suspicious outsiders in the lobby and in other areas of the building such as the corridors and recreation room constitutes both a violation of expected ways in which these areas are supposed to be used and an invasion of territorial limits that could involve harm to the elderly residents. The right to enter the building is a privilege extended only to those who have legitimate personal or official business there. Strangers are viewed as potential assailants who may rob or physically harm tenants who happen to be near.

6. Sommer (1969) states that "in many situations, defense of personal space is so entangled with defense of an immediate territory that one sees these as part of a single process—the defense of privacy" (45). Many of the St. Regis residents place a high premium on their personal privacy. Solitary lifestyles, reclusive drinking patterns, and desire to preserve secrecy in daily activities serve to intensify efforts to protect the boundaries of individual apartments against unwanted intrusions. Concerns for privacy are also increased by the circumstance of living under crowded conditions in a high-rise structure where personal control over unwanted encounters with other occupants is limited.

In a setting where the maintenance of residential status is predicated on ability to function independently, maintaining public impressions of personal competence assumes critical importance. Behind the privacy of locked doors, one can relax and "be old." Dentures can be removed, uncomfortable girdles can be discarded, and makeup can be taken off without concern for preserving the appearance of a more youthful, capable self. Thus, desire for privacy, as well as for safety, adds to the motivation to protect the sanctity of individual apartments.

7. The actual truth of this incident is questionable because I was never able to determine the names of those involved. But the story itself illustrates how the carrying of guns is not regarded as a surprising or unusual practice in a neighborhood where criminal attacks happen frequently. No one remarked on the fact that it was improper to be carrying a gun in the first place.

8. In his article "Victimization in Old Age," Gubrium (1974) distinguishes between concern about crime and fear of victimization. *Con-*

cern about crime he defines more objectively as referring to generalized attitudes toward existing crime rates and the social conditions that affect the extent of criminal victimization. *Fear* he defines as relating more directly to subjective feelings about the possibilities of being criminally assaulted.

Appendix

1. Gouldner (1971) comments on the importance of the reflexive character of methodological descriptions: "The inquiring subject and the studied object are seen not only as mutually interrelated but also as mutually constituted. . . . The social world, therefore, is to be known not simply by 'discovery' of some external fact, not only by looking outward, but also by opening oneself inward. . . . For there is no knowledge of the world that is not a knowledge of our own experiences with it and our relation to it" (493).

2. There is considerable ambiguity in the literature regarding precise definitions of the role of participant observer and the method of participant observation (Gold 1958; McCall and Simons 1969; Reiss 1954). These terms are often used interchangeably with field research, field observation, and qualitative observation and encompass a variety of investigative strategies. Methods can range over formal and informal interviewing, participant and nonparticipant observation of ongoing events, documentary analyses, and structured questionnaires. In my study, *participant observation* is used in the broader sense and encompasses the diverse methods that I used in obtaining data.

3. For a full discussion of "nonreactive" strategies in field research, see Webb et al. (1966).

4. In other investigations field workers have been variously viewed as a covert investigator for a government agency (James 1961), a communist spy, and a threat to the existing power structure (Diamond 1964; Vidich and Bensman 1968) as well as confidante and friend (Gans 1965; Hannerz 1969; Whyte 1955).

5. This difficulty was also recognized by some members of the Housing Authority staff. On one occasion the receptionist remarked that she was careful not to become too attached to some of the tenants because of the frequent occurrence of death. Similar feelings were expressed to me

by some of the medical personnel in a convalescent home where I was involved in research (Smithers 1977). Such attitudes are similar to avoidance practices often operative when someone is designated as terminally ill, and they can be described as a type of anticipatory distancing that reduces the possibilities of painful grieving when death occurs.

References

Adams, J. S. 1963. "Towards an Understanding of Inequity." *Journal of Abnormal and Social Psychology* 67:422–436.

Atchley, R. 1980. *The Social Forces in Later Life.* Belmont, Calif.: Wadsworth.

Becker, H., and B. Greer. 1957. "Participant Observation and Interviewing: A Comparison." *Human Organization* 16:28–35.

Berkowitz, L. 1972. "Social Norms, Feelings and Other Factors Affecting Helping and Altruism." In L. Berkowitz (ed.), *Advances in Experimental Social Psychology,* 6:63–108. New York: Academic.

Berkowitz, L., and P. Friedman. 1967. "Some Social Class Differences in Helping Behaviors." *Journal of Personality and Social Psychology* 5:217–225.

Biklen, D. 1979. "The Case for Deinstitutionalization." *Social Policy* 9:48–54.

Bild, D., and R. Havighurst. 1976. "Senior Citizens in Great Cities: The Case of Chicago." *Gerontologist* 16, pt. II.

Birren, J. E. 1970. "Abuse of the Urban Aged." *Psychology Today* 3:37–38.

Blau, P. 1955. *The Dynamics of Bureaucracy.* Chicago: University of Chicago Press.

———. 1964. *Exchange and Power in Social Life.* New York: Wiley.

Braungart, M. M., W. J. Hoyer, and R. G. Braungart. 1979. "Fear of Crime and the Elderly." In A. P. Goldstein, W. J. Hoyer, and P. J. Monti (eds.), *Police and the Elderly,* 142–163. New York: Pergamon.

Brice, D. 1970. "The Geriatric Ghetto." *San Francisco* 12:70–72.

Campbell, D. T. 1955. "The Informant in Quantitative Research." *American Journal of Sociology* 60:339–342.

Cantor, M. H. 1975. "Life Space and the Social Support Systems of the Inner City Elderly of New York." *Gerontologist* 15:58–66.

Cantor, M. H., and M. Mayer. 1976. "Health and the Inner City Elderly." *Gerontologist* 16:17–25.

Clark, M. 1971. "Patterns of Aging among the Elderly Poor of the Inner City." *Gerontologist* 11:58–66.

Clemente, F., and M. Kleinman. 1976. "Fear of Crime among the Aged." *Gerontologist* 16:207–210.

Cohen, C., and J. Sokolovsky. 1980. "Social Engagement versus Isolation: The Case of the Aged in SRO Hotels." *Gerontologist* 20:36–44.

Cook, F. L., W. G. Skogan, T. D. Cook, and G. E. Antunes. 1978. "Criminal Victimization of the Elderly: The Physical and Economic Consequences." *Gerontologist* 18:338–349.

Daniels, L. R., and L. Berkowitz. 1963. "Liking and Response to Dependency Relationships." *Human Relations* 16:141–148.

Diamond, S. 1964. "Nigerian Discovery: The Politics of Field Work." In A. J. Vidich, J. Bensman, and M. Stein (eds.), *Reflections on Community Studies,* 119–154. New York: Wiley.

Dowd, J. J. 1980. "Exchange Rates and Old People." *Journal of Gerontology* 35:596–602.

Eckert, J. K. 1979a. "The Social Ecology of SRO Living." *Generations* 3 (Winter):22–23.

———. 1979b. "Urban Renewal and Redevelopment: High Risk for the Marginally Subsistent Elderly." *Gerontologist* 19:496–502.

———. 1980. *The Unseen Elderly: A Study of Marginally Subsistent Hotel Dwellers.* San Diego: Campanile Press, San Diego State University.

Ehrlich, P. 1976. "St. Louis 'Invisible' Elderly Needs and Characteristics of Aged 'Single Room Occupancy' Downtown Hotel Residents." St. Louis: Institute of Applied Gerontology, St. Louis University.

Ehrlich, P., I. Ehrlich, and P. Woehlke. 1982. "Congregate Housing for the Elderly: Thirteen Years Later." *Gerontologist* 22:399–403.

Erickson, R. J., and J. K. Eckert. 1977. "The Elderly Poor in Downtown San Diego Hotels." *Gerontologist* 17:440–446.

Festinger, L. 1954. "A Theory of Social Comparison Processes." *Human Relations* 5:117–140.

Fischer, C. S. 1973. "On Urban Alienation and Anomie: Powerlessness, Social Isolation." *American Sociological Review* 38:311–326.

Francis, D. G. 1981. "Adaptive Strategies of the Elderly." In C. Fry and contributors, *Dimensions: Aging, Culture and Health*, 205–222. New York: Bergin.

Fry, C. 1979. "Structural Conditions Affecting Community Formation among the Aged: Two Examples from Arizona." *Anthropological Quarterly* 52:7–17.

Gans, H. J. 1965. *The Urban Villagers*. New York: Free Press.

Gergen, K., S. Morse, and K. Bode. 1974. "Overpaid or overworked? Cognitive and Behavioral Reactions to Inequitable Rewards." *Journal of Applied Social Psychology* 4:259–274.

Goffman, E. 1967. *Interaction Ritual: Essays on Face-to-Face Behavior*. New York: Doubleday.

Golant, S. M. 1975. "Residential Concentration of the Future Elderly." *Gerontologist* 15:16–23.

————. 1979. "Central City, Suburban and Nonmetropolitan Migration Patterns of the Elderly." In S. M. Golant (ed.), *Location and Environment of the Elderly Population*, 37–54. New York: Wiley.

Gold, R. 1958. "Roles in Sociological Field Observation." *Social Forces* 36:217–223.

Goldsmith, J., and S. Goldsmith. 1976. *Crime and the Elderly*. Lexington Mass.: Heath.

Gouldner, A. W. 1966. "The Norm of Reciprocity: A Preliminary Statement." In B. J. Biddle and E. Thomas (eds.), *Role Theory: Concepts and Research*, 136–144. New York: Wiley.

————. 1971. *The Coming Crisis of Western Sociology*. New York: Avon.

Greenberg, M., and S. P. Shapiro. 1971. "Indebtedness: An Adverse Aspect of Asking for and Receiving Help." *Sociometry* 34:290–301.

Gross, A., and B. Latane. 1974. "Receiving Help, Reciprocation and Interpersonal Attraction." *Journal of Applied Social Psychology* 3:210–223.

Gubrium, J. F. 1974. "Victimization in Old Age." *Crime and Delinquency* 20:245–250.

————. 1975. "Being Single in Old Age." *International Journal of Aging and Human Development* 6:29–41.

Hannerz, U. 1969. *Soulside: Inquiries into Ghetto Culture and Community.* New York: Columbia University Press.

Hertz, E., and O. Hutheesing. 1975. "At the Edge of Society: The Nominal Culture of Urban Hotel Isolates." *Urban Anthropology* 4:317–332.

Hochschild, A. R. 1973. *The Unexpected Community.* Englewood Cliffs, N.J.: Prentice-Hall.

Homans, G. 1958. "Social Behavior as Exchange." *American Journal of Sociology* 62:597–606.

Housing Authority Security Guard Reports, 1976, 1977.

Isenberg, B. 1972. "Out to Pasture: To Be Old and Poor Is To Be Alone, Afraid and Ill-Fed." *Wall Street Journal,* November 15, 1–2.

Jackson, J. J. 1980. *Minorities and Aging.* Belmont, Calif.: Wadsworth.

James, R. 1961. "A Note on Phases of the Community Role of the Participant Observer." *American Sociological Review* 21:446–450.

Johnson, J. 1975. *Doing Field Research.* New York: Free Press.

Johnson, S. K. 1971. *Idle Haven: Community Building among the Working-Class Retired.* Berkeley and Los Angeles: University of California Press.

Jonas, K., and E. Wellin. 1981. "Dependency and Reciprocity: Home Health Aid in an Elderly Population." In C. Fry and contributors, *Dimensions: Aging, Culture and Health,* 111–132. New York: Bergin.

Kahana, E. 1982. "Congruence Model of Person–Environment Interaction." In M. P. Lawton, P. G. Windley, and T. O. Byerts (eds.), *Aging and the Environment: Theoretical Approaches,* 97–121. New York: Springer.

Kalish, R. A. 1967. "Of Children and Grandfathers: A Speculative Essay on Dependency." *Gerontologist* 7:65–69.

Kandel, R. F., and M. Heider. 1979. "Friendship and Factionalism in a Tri-ethnic Housing Complex for the Elderly in North Miami." *Anthropological Quarterly* 52:49–57.

Kasl, S. 1972. "Physical and Mental Health Effects of Involuntary

Relocation and Institutionalization on the Elderly: A Review."
American Journal of Public Health 62:377–383.

Kastler, M., R. M. Gray, and M. L. Carruty. 1968. "Involuntary
Relocation of the Elderly." *Journal of Gerontology* 8:276–279.

Krebs, D. L. 1970. "Altruism: An Examination of the Concept and
a Review of the Literature." *Psychological Bulletin* 73:258–
302.

Lally, M., E. Black, M. Thornock, and J. D. Hawkins. 1979. "Older
Women in Single Room Occupant (SRO) Hotels: A Seattle Profile." *Gerontologist* 19:67–73.

Lanzetta, J. Y. 1958."Group Behavior under Stress." *Human Relations*
8:29–52.

Latane, B., and J. M. Darley. 1970. *The Unresponsive Bystander: Why
Doesn't He Help?* New York: Appleton, Century, Crofts.

Lawton, M. P., M. Greenbaum, and B. Liebowitz. 1980. "The
Lifespan of Housing Environments for the Aged." *Gerontologist*
20:56–64.

Lawton, M. P., and S. Yaffe. 1980. "Victimization and Fear of Crime
in Elderly Public Housing Tenants." *Journal of Gerontology*
35:768–779.

Lichter, D. T., G. V. Fuguitt, T. B. Heaton, and W. B. Clifford.
1981. "Components of Change in the Residential Concentration
of the Elderly Population: 1950–1975." *Journal of Gerontology*
36:480–489.

Lopata, H. Z. 1975. "Support Systems of Elderly Urbanites: Chicago of
the 1970's." *Gerontologist* 5:35–41.

Lyman, S., and M. B. Scott. 1967. "Territoriality: A Neglected Sociological Dimension." *Social Problems* 15:236–249.

McCall, G. S., and J. L. Simmons. 1969. *Issues in Participant Observation.* Reading, Mass.: Addison-Wesley.

Merton, R. 1947. "Selected Problems of Field Work in a Planned
Community." *American Sociological Review* 12:104–112.

Midlarsky, E. 1971. "Aiding under Stress: The Effects of Competence,
Dependency, Visibility and Fatalism." *Journal of Personality*
39:132–149.

Newman, O. 1972. *Defensible Space: Crime Prevention through Urban Design.* New York: Macmillan, Collier Books.

Park, R. E., and W. Burgess, eds. 1925. *The City.* Chicago: University of Chicago Press.

Rainwater, L. 1966. "Fear and the House-as-Haven in the Lower Class." *American Institute of Planners* 32:23–31.

Reiss, A. J., Jr. 1954. "Some Logical and Methodological Problems in Community Research." *Social Forces* 33:52–54.

Rosenberg, G. S. 1968. "Age, Poverty and Isolation from Friends in the Urban Working Class." *Journal of Gerontology* 23:533–538.

Rosow, I. 1967. *Social Integration of the Aged.* Toronto: Collier-Macmillan Canada.

Ross, J.-K. 1977. *Old People New Lives: Community Creation in a Retirement Residence.* Chicago: University of Chicago Press.

Rowles, G. D. 1981. "The Surveillance Zone as Meaningful Space for the Aged." *Gerontologist* 21:304–311.

Schopler, J., and M. W. Matthews. 1965. "The Influence of the Perceived Causal Locus of Partner's Dependence on the Use of Interpersonal Power." *Journal of Personality and Social Psychology* 2:609–612.

Shapiro, J. H. 1971. *Communities of the Alone.* New York: Association Press.

Sherif, M., O. J. Harvey, B. J. White, W. R. Hood, and C. W. Sherif. 1961. *Intergroup Conflict and Cooperation: The Robbers' Cave Experiment.* Norman, Okla.: University Book Exchange.

Sherman, E., E. S. Newman, A. Nelson, and D. Van Buren. 1975. *Crimes against the Elderly in Public Housing: Policy Alternatives.* Albany: School of Social Welfare, State University of New York at Albany.

Sherman, S. 1975a. "Mutual Assistance and Support in Retirement Housing." *Journal of Gerontology* 30:479–483.

———. 1975b. "Patterns of Contacts for Residents of Age-segregated and Age-integrated Housing." *Journal of Gerontology* 30:103–107.

Siegal, H. 1978. *Outposts of the Forgotten.* New Brunswick, N.J.: Transaction.

Simmel, G. 1950. *The Sociology of Georg Simmel.* Ed. K. H. Wolff. Glencoe, Ill.: Free Press.

Smithers, J. A. 1977. "Institutional Dimensions of Senility." *Urban Life* 6:251–276.

Sokolovsky, J., and C. Cohen. 1978. "The Cultural Meaning of Personal Networks for the Inner-city Elderly." *Urban Anthropology* 7:323–341.

————.1981. "Measuring Social Interaction of the Urban Elderly: A Methodological Synthesis." *International Journal of Aging and Human Development* 13:223–244.

Sommer, R. 1969. *Personal Space: The Behavioral Basis of Design.* Englewood Cliffs, N.J.: Prentice-Hall.

Stephens, J. 1974. "Romance in the SRO: Relationships of Elderly Men and Women in a Slum Hotel." *Gerontologist* 14:279–282.

————.1976. *Loners, Lovers and Losers: Elderly Tenants in a Slum Hotel.* Seattle: University of Washington Press.

Sunderland, G., M. Cose, and S. Stiles. 1980. *Law Enforcement and Older Persons.* Washington, D.C.: Law Enforcement Assistance Administration.

Suttles, G. D. 1972. *The Social Construction of Communities.* Chicago: University of Chicago Press.

Suttles, G. D., and D. Street. 1970. "Aid to the Poor and Social Exchange." In E. O. Laumann, P. M. Siegel, and R. W. Hodge (eds.), *The Logic of Social Hierarchies,* 744–755. Chicago: Markham.

Tissue, T. L. 1971. "Old Age, Poverty and the Central City." *Aging and Human Development* 2:235–248.

U.S. Bureau of the Census. 1970. *Census of Population and Housing, Census Tracts, Los Angeles.* No. 117. Washington, D.C.: GPO.

U.S. Bureau of the Census. 1980. *Census of Population and Housing, Census Tracts, Los Angeles.* No. 226. Washington, D.C.: GPO.

U.S. Department of Justice. 1976. "Criminal Victimization in the United States: A Comparison of 1973 and 1974 Findings." Washington, D.C.: National Criminal Justice Information and Statistics Services, Law Enforcement Assistance Administration.

————.1979. *Mutual Concern: Older Americans and the Criminal Justice System.* National Institute of Law Enforcement and Criminal Justice, Law Enforcement Assistance Administration, Washington, D.C.: GPO.

U.S. Senate, Special Committee on Aging. 1978. "Single Room Occupancy: A Need for National Concern." Washington, D.C.: GPO.

Vidal, A., and G. Shapiro. 1955. "A Comparison of Participant Observation and Survey Data." *American Sociological Review* 20:28–33.

Vidich, A. J., and J. Bensman. 1968. *Small Town in Mass Society.* Princeton, N.J.: Princeton University Press.

Webb, E. J., D. T. Campbell, R. D. Schwartz, and L. Sechrest. 1966. *Unobtrusive Measures: Nonreactive Research in the Social Sciences.* Chicago: Rand-McNally.

Wellin, E., and E. Boyer. 1979. "Adjustments of Black and White Elderly to the Same Adaptive Niche." *Anthropological Quarterly* 52:39–48.

Wentowski, G. J. 1981. "Reciprocity and the Coping Strategies of Older People: Cultural Dimensions of Network Building." *Gerontologist* 21:600–605.

Whyte, W. F. 1955. *Street Corner Society.* Chicago: University of Chicago Press.

Wirth, L. 1938. "Urbanism as a Way of Life." *American Journal of Sociology* 44:1–24.

Wolfenberger, W. 1972. *The Principle of Normalization in Human Services.* Toronto: National Institute on Mental Retardation.

Yancey, W. L. 1973. "Architecture, Interaction and Social Control: The Case of a Large Scale Public Housing Project." In J. Helmer and N. A. Eddington (eds.), *Urban Man: The Psychology of Urban Survival,* 107–122. New York: Free Press.

Zorbaugh, H. 1926. "Dwellers in Furnished Rooms: An Urban Type." In E. W. Burgess (ed.), *The Urban Community,* 98–105. Chicago: University of Chicago Press.

Index